Ken Knight has been writing since his desk was pushed across the hall from Grade 3 to 4 and as part of various careers since then. A life-long resident of Calgary, Knight enjoys writing more than any other thing and creates a poem, story or song every year for his family Christmas card, which includes all the year's news in rhyme.

For Les, my partner in this anxious life. May we continue to dream together and never stop believing it 'will' get better.

Ken Knight

Thru the Blue and Happy Too

Austin Macauley Publishers™

LONDON · CAMBRIDGE · NEW YORK · SHARJAH

Copyright © Ken Knight (2019)

The right of Ken Knight to be identified as author of this work has been asserted by him in accordance with section 77 and 78 of the Copyright, Designs and Patents Act 1988.

All rights reserved. No part of this publication may be reproduced, stored in a retrieval system, or transmitted in any form or by any means, electronic, mechanical, photocopying, recording, or otherwise, without the prior permission of the publishers.

Any person who commits any unauthorized act in relation to this publication may be liable to criminal prosecution and civil claims for damages.

A CIP catalogue record for this title is available from the British Library.

ISBN 9781528920858 (Paperback)
ISBN 9781528920865 (Hardback)
ISBN 9781528963220 (ePub e-book)

www.austinmacauley.com

First Published (2019)
Austin Macauley Publishers Ltd
25 Canada Square
Canary Wharf
London
E14 5LQ

One man's journey through an anxious life

Introduction

My first book, *Lefty Loosey Righty Tighty,* was written as a bit of a guide book to my daughters as they left the nest and went out into this big crazy world on their own. As I started to interact with my girls as adults, I realized they had developed a lot of the same anxieties as I had. But let's be clear – I am the king of anxiety and my kingdom will not be overthrown!

I don't profess to be a professional, a doctor, a psychologist or a therapist. I certainly have had no formal training in these fields unless you count one university child psychology class I took in the early 1980s to fill a gap in my schedule!

What I have had is some personal experience. Experience with living a pretty great life but with extreme anxiety and fear following me around with every step for a whole lot of years. Have I been cured? Absolutely not. Will this book cure you? Likely not. My hope is this book will make you realize that many of us have anxiety and fears and we can still carry on with a pretty fantastic life experience.

My hope is that by providing anecdotal examples and stories from my own life, you can relate and realize we are all on the same basic path. I am no guru. I'm just a guy, a son, a dad and a husband that suffers and has found a few helpful tips along the way. I find many books on this subject have lost me in their pages and I give up. But if you can read this on your coffee break, at the bus stop, before you turn out the light or, my favourite, in the bathroom, I have been successful.

I will share some tips and tricks I learned along the way to minimize my anxiety – or at least make light of it. I don't want this to be another stress for you. Some books I pick up, I have to put down because I start getting anxious about reading about anxiety!

A few years ago, there were many books and videos surrounding the concept of 'it gets better'. The intent was generally for older more experienced people to tell younger people that they should be patient for that time of life when it does, in fact, get better. And the bigger message was to encourage them – maybe even beg them – to not try to end their lives prematurely.

I am a walking and talking example of how it gets better. So read on and let's get started.

The Ills
Those Bothersome Things

1
In the Beginning

As early in my life as I can remember, I was convinced I was a retard. I'm sorry, but they did actually call people retards back then, you know – in the 1960s. Kids said unkind things and there was no such thing as political correctness in those days. And so, I thought I was a retard, mentally challenged or slow – whatever you want to call it.

I thought my parents were just too kind – or afraid – to tell me, that everyone was playing along and was operating under some kind of promise that I was not to find out. My mom would tell those cute stories at family gatherings about how I always fell out of my crib as a baby and landed on my head. This added fuel to the verdict. I obviously had a severe head injury.

So on one hand, I had clearly developed the lowest possible self-image at a very young age and, on the other, my entire universe was apparently executing a finely-managed plan to avoid bringing to light my mental incapacities. Complicated!

As the years passed, I gradually realized that I was perhaps not mentally challenged and there was no grand plan to hide it from me. I started to do extremely well at my school work and couldn't keep believing that it too was a charade for my benefit.

But fear and anxiety of imaginary problems have been my companions for most of my life. It seems as though as one chapter ended and another started, I brought along a fresh new fear.

2
The Big Push

In fact, because I was perceived by the education system to be somewhat gifted, on a cold snowy day in November of the third grade, my desk was pushed across the hallway of our elementary school and I was instantly in the fourth grade. The new class was learning how to write capital Gs in script that day. My friends Debbie and Jeffrey had been 'accelerated' along with me and we all settled into our G-writing tasks quickly.

Jumping ahead a grade is not without its consequences, however, and no doubt one of the reasons it rarely occurs in the present day, especially without ever asking or advising one's parents! You can imagine my mother's surprise when I came home from school that afternoon with the news of my new grade status.

I instantly became the youngest and smallest grade-four boy in the school and this of course carried on throughout my school days to follow. Many years later, I was one of the youngest kids at university, taking my entire first year of studies as a seventeen-year-old.

And so, while my retard days were behind me – and no one had ever actually called me that to my face – the days were now filled with childhood taunts of being called a fairy, wimp and later, a faggot. That was the popular terminology of the day in the mid-1970s.

Looking back, it is very weird that calling someone a fag even had any meaning. Some people in the United Kingdom still refer to cigarettes as fags. But back then, there were no television or movie personalities that were known to be gay and certainly the subject matter was not popular. In fact, in the place I grew up, it was still illegal to be gay.

So I guess using the term fag was somehow construed to be a perfectly horrible thing to say and a good choice when you were bullying a kid smaller and younger than yourself.

Horrible it was and it worked. I was afraid to go to school, afraid to go to the playground at recess and especially afraid to participate in sports or activities in gym class.

3
Gym Jitters

Ah yes, gym class, or physical education as it is now called, unless they have come up with a new moniker. That special part of one's schooling that is absolutely designed to separate the weak from the strong, the introverts from the extroverts and the bullies from the bullied. And the perfect chance to put everyone in a locker room to disrobe and show off their adolescent muscles or, in my case, skinny arms and ribs that would not stay hidden inside my skin.

Once adorned in our fashionable gym strip, as it was called, it was then time to line up and be chosen for one side or the other of opposing teams for everything from soccer to dodge ball. And of course, to make it absolutely perfect, only the strongest and best and at each sport were assigned to do the choosing in order to guarantee the skinny, scared runts like me were chosen last and with a fair degree of disappointment on the part of the chooser.

Then it was time for the gym teacher to step back and let the chaos ensue. There is no need to actually explain how the sport was played or take any time to show some basic skills to the uninformed. Let the natural order of things proceed – those already stronger and better to conquer and, in the process, annihilate the wimps.

I eventually found my way through this daily torture by finding an activity at which I was actually competent – the 100-metre hurdles. It was great because it was not a team sport and I could run and jump faster than anyone else. All that practice of being chased home from school had finally paid off. I eventually even won the city championships. It certainly didn't make me better at any of the other sports, but at least I could say I had excelled at one activity!

I am pretty sure today's schools have figured out how to be a little more understanding of the diversity of skills in a class, but I cannot guarantee it. What I know for sure, as it worked for me, is to not worry about all the things you aren't good at in gym class and focus on what you are. And not to belittle the gym teachers out there, but as long as they have one good thing to write on your report card, they will probably leave you alone.

4
It Got Worse

In the sixth grade, things actually got worse for me. I'll never know if it was puberty starting to emerge in my classmates or just a continuation of my being the smallest and youngest and an easy target. And despite being moved ahead a grade, there were still a few of us at the top of the class academically, which further divided us.

The taunting and bullying had gotten worse and one day I snapped. I started screaming at one girl – Belinda – who was making fun of me for something I have long since forgotten. It was a bit like an out-of-body experience, a little version of me having a melt-down in the middle of a classroom of kids and somehow watching it all take place from some imaginary camera location high above.

When I was done with my outburst, I went and hid in the boys' washroom. I am not really sure how long I was in there, but I imagine some teacher or administrator finally came along and coaxed me out and sent me home.

Upon learning of the incident, my parents – bless their hearts – decided to enrol me in Tae Kwon-Do classes (a Korean martial art) to give me a thicker skin and the ability to defend myself. Please do not ever do this to your children! The result was one more activity where I was singled out as smaller and weaker than other students. I also had to keep the classes a secret out of fear that the bullies at school would find out and challenge me to a fight to test my newfound skills.

The trouble with fear, especially when it involves something like bullying, is you believe something bad is going to happen to you. There is no doubt I was taunted, called bad names and chased home from school. But I was never actually physically harmed.

So we know fear is an unpleasant emotion caused by the belief that someone or something is dangerous, threatening or likely to cause pain. We need to remember the 'belief' word in that sentence. Fear is caused by a belief. A belief is an acceptance that something is true and actually exists. So if fear is merely a belief and a belief is simply an acceptance, can't we accept a new belief? The instant I did, things started to change in my life for the better. The biggest challenge is recognizing fear for what it is, and knowing an actual fear is never as scary as the ones you imagine.

5
A Fresh Start

The transition between the sixth and seventh grade usually means a change of schools, at least in Canada, from elementary to junior high. Because of my past history with the bully crowd, I begged my parents to let me go to a different junior high than most of my classmates. Two of my closest friends had moved away and were not going to be going to that school anyway. Running away certainly seemed the best option for my worries and troubles.

For whatever reason, I started the seventh grade at the neighbourhood designated school anyway and was destined to 'make the best of it'. And surprisingly, that's exactly what happened.

For what seemed like forever, I had wanted to join the school band and learn to play the flute. The band teacher was, let's just say, not very competent and when I could not make a sound on the flute on my first attempt, she assigned me to the drums. And that one moment ended up shaping my musical life for many years to come.

I loved playing the drums and all the various percussion instruments that went along with it. I took private lessons and soon was pretty good. Although the band teacher was 'reassigned' mid-way through that year, I ended up doing something I loved and being a part of a group of really great kids.

Another group of really great kids were my friends, which were all mostly girls. My mom called them my harem. We were all at the top of the class academically and, when away from school, had a lot of good clean fun.

So while the kids that had once bullied me were still around, I now had my own interests and friends and it didn't seem to matter anymore. There's a tip in there somewhere.

Playing the drums and band became a major outlet for me, and when I joined a local marching band, it also became my first introduction to overseas travel and I was hooked.

The great thing about playing in a band is how everyone is responsible for just one thing – their own piece of music. And when everyone plays their part, the result is a beautiful composition. A metaphor for life? Absolutely.

I also joined the high school yearbook club and photography club where this same principle shone through. I got to work on a small piece of something bigger, where no one judged how much or how little each other contributed as long as we all worked together.

For this young, skinny, introverted boy, being a part of a band and joining clubs were the magic formula to relieve my fears and I highly recommend it.

6
People Power

As I write these words, a phenomenon is taking place in the western world. Under the banner of the words, "Me too", women are coming forward by the thousands to accuse men of sexual assault and harassment, especially in the workplace. Some men have joined the cause as well with their own stories of abuse and harassment.

No human being should be abused by another and it is time this ended for good. In fact, there is an organization that has now formed under the banner *Time's Up*. I think we can all agree the workplace has enough pressures and stress, so we do not need to add fear of sexual harassment to the mix.

I hesitated to even write this chapter because the issue is so heated and so very personal. But since we are talking about worry and anxiety, I wanted to share both my own history and a perspective that might possibly be worth considering.

What makes it hard to be liberal and write a chapter that supports the understanding of boys and men is running the absolute risk you will be called anti-female and sexist. So of course like anything in this book, I encourage you to use the shopping-cart method – if you're not buying it, move on!

After almost forty years in the workforce, I can say that I have worked for all kinds of bosses, but I have had female and male bosses almost equally over those years. I would say that as supervisors go, men and women rank about even for me. Some were hands-on and some were hands-off – and I mean that in terms of their management approach and not their actual hands! My managers were also either really good at providing recognition and coaching or really bad at it.

Where my experiences – and therefore my views – might swing to the other side is how men who are fathers or caregivers are treated by society and the workplace. I have watched, for most of my career, women call in sick, arrive late and leave early to take care of their children, whether that is for medical appointments, to attend activities or volunteer at the school.

But as a father wanting to do these same things, it was (and still is) completely frowned upon and, in some cases, outright forbidden. And I know from all the mothers who have either worked with me or been my colleagues over the years that the fathers of their children do not even consider undertaking these activities for the same reasons. Someone decided this is 'women's work'.

As someone divorced from my children's mother, I also know first-hand about father's rights when a marriage comes to an end. There is probably no other area in which men and women's treatment is quite so out of balance.

With a documented anti-father bias in the court system, many fathers are actually showing symptoms of post-traumatic stress disorder when they lose access to their children, or at the very least, they suffer major anxiety. Statistics Canada says 96 percent of child support orders in Canada are made against fathers and almost 78 percent of sole custody orders are granted to mothers.

I was one of these dads. After proposing that their mother and I share our time with the girls equally, I was completely shut down and only allowed to see my daughters every second weekend – and one two-hour dinner in between. And, I had to make sure I sent thousands of dollars over punctually on the first of every month or be dragged back into court. Sounds fair?

I had been the guy who, each night after a full day's work, had fed them, bathed them, read stories to them, did homework with them and eventually collapsed asleep with them, and was now some kind of second-class citizen with 'visitation rights'. And before you suggest their mother was doing the same, it might help to know she did not work outside the home and I also spent the better part of my weekends cleaning the house.

As I have already stated, this is not intended to be an attack on women or even the particular woman to which I used to be married. I am merely stating the facts of my particular case and one which I know to be quite common.

I left the marriage with my car and my clothes, leaving her with a million-dollar home, furnishings and art, a car and a substantial wad of cash. The monthly child support payments – which incidentally she did not have to claim as income for tax purposes and I could not claim as a deduction – were squandered on purchases like artificial grass and online shopping while the kids arrived at my house for their weekend visit without new underwear or jeans.

While the courts were clear on what had to happen when the marriage ended, there was absolutely no mechanism to ensure things stayed on track thereafter.

Redemption came several years later when my daughters decided on their own to come and live with me and my partner, Les, and, since their ages now permitted this in the court's eyes, it was a relatively seamless transition. And what it further proved was that the two parents had truly been somewhat equal all along, despite a flawed system.

My purpose here is not to start a debate about the perils of divorce among parents or the dysfunctionality of the court system. What I am proposing is that we all stop trying to make the man-woman thing a competition, whether in the workplace or at home. Since we are all just *people* with different private parts and abilities to bear offspring, can we not just call it even and move on?

I know what I propose may be too simplistic for some people, but much of what I have written in these pages is pretty simple stuff. And if some sort of gender-based conflict is keeping you awake at night or giving you an ulcer, it might just be worth considering.

7
Clutter Confuses

I grew up in a home that was pretty well-organized, especially considering my parents raised three children in it and it was only 800 square feet, plus a basement. The old adage of 'a place for everything and everything in its place' definitely applied. Inside, my mother made sure everything was organized and neat. In the garage, I remember rows and rows of neatly-arranged jars of screws and nails my father had fashioned to keep everything in order.

It was a bit of a tough transition for me, therefore, when I discovered the complete chaos in which my first spouse and her family lived. When we went to my then-parents in-law's home for dinner, the job somehow always became mine to set the dining room table. I didn't mind this task at all, except that I would always have to first *find* the dining room table. It would be piled high with newspapers, magazines, unopened mail and, often, the clean pots and dishes from the last family dinner that had not been put away.

In their double-car garage, there was so much stuff; they could only barely squeeze one car into it. The remainder was crammed with old newspapers, keepsakes and long-forgotten tools and camping equipment.

I found this disorganization very stressful and, since the very definition of the word *disorganization* includes 'lack of control', it made me very uncomfortable. Most of us human beings thrive in a state of peace and calm, control and organization.

You may not even realize your environment is causing you anxiety. And there are plenty of 'reality' television shows that make light of this and also minimize the effort it takes to overcome being buried in your own clutter. Trust me, you cannot relax and find peace if you cannot find a place to sit down.

So if you have a bit of chaos causing you anxiety and you haven't been lucky enough to have won a complete home makeover, my advice is to start small and work slowly through your space to improve it.

My pantry is organized into bins and jars for flour, sugar, nuts, pasta and many other things and each one has a label. It saves time when you are cooking and helps you avoid the nasty mistake of picking the wrong look-alike ingredient. It's easy to see when you are running low on something and when you do come home with more, it's easy to find the right place to put it. And it avoids a big jumble of half-full bags and boxes falling on your head every time you disrupt the ecosystem.

Pick a room at a time or even go smaller – a drawer or a closet at a time – and straighten out the contents. I'm a fan of removing everything, going through it and then replacing only what is still needed or wanted. This is a good time to give the drawer or closet a good vacuum or washing as well. Then you will have room for a whole bunch more stuff that might be lying around the house in need of a resting spot. But resist the temptation to just fill them up again with more unneeded things!

If you have small children, their toys and games can overwhelm a space in a matter of minutes, so make sure you have some big containers or bins in which to collect them after playtime. And this is a great time to teach the kids whose job it is to pick up their toys.

One of the ways to reduce the paper coming into your home is to sign up for paperless delivery of all your bank statements, bills and subscriptions. Many people read the daily newspaper online now and that not only saves a few trees but keeps all that extra paper out of your home. Using your own reusable shopping bags also keeps disposable bags from piling up and, in many places, is now mandatory.

8
Disastrous Dates

Back in the 1970s when I met the girl that was to later become my wife, dating was somewhat simpler. We went to the same high school, had many of the same friends and took band class together. What started out as friendship grew stronger. We went to graduation together and the rest is history, so to speak.

By the time twenty-five years had passed and I had come out of the closet and ended that marriage, dating had completely changed – not to mention that I was now a man seeking a man! I did not belong to any social groups in which I could meet people and, with only a couple of hidden-away bars in my backward-thinking town, not a lot of places to meet people either.

The internet was alive and well, however, with a few scattered sites for both straight and gay singles to connect. As with anything in life, there were online scammers who were – and looked – nothing like their profiles when it came time to actually meet. What's that old saying? "You have to kiss a lot of frogs to find your prince."

My most memorable date was at a local McDonald's restaurant – his choice – where he ordered two full meals for himself. It was 9:00 p.m. at night. Not really knowing what to order myself, I had an apple pie. The conversation eventually turned to my young children, with which he said he could never be involved and certainly expected to be at the top of the list over them. Finish pie. End of date.

Bad dates are anxiety-causing agony. If my McDonald's date is at one end of the spectrum, then perhaps watching three hours of community theatre in a church basement is at the other. Then there's the inevitable conversation about how the last boyfriend wronged them – or you – or even worse, no conversation at all beyond how your day was at work and the change in the weather today.

The good news, of course, is Les and I eventually met on one of those early dating sites, fell instantly in love and the rest, once again, is history.

Fast forward another twelve years and dating has morphed into another completely different realm. Dating apps for our mobile devices are available by the hundreds. Combined with all the other time we spend on social media, gaming and news sites, they can suck hours out of your day. And how about *that* anxiety?

Choosing the right photo for your profile and writing the perfect profile for yourself – stressful! We are sold an imagined place where everyone and everything is perfect, with a sea of stress-free matches and guaranteed dates. What we get in reality, however, is endless small talk with people who really don't want to get off their couch and actually do anything or meet anyone.

We have created a world where it's really easy to meet people, but almost impossible to actually connect. It's just not the "I met him at church" or "we grew up together on the same street" situation of the past.

What I am recommending is an end – or at least a hiatus – to anxiety dating. Stop worrying about finding Mr. or Mrs. Right and freaking out when there are 'no matches' for you on your phone. Maybe if you take that cooking class or golf lesson you have been putting off, the 'right' person will be standing beside you or winking at you from across the room or green.

9
Pressure Cooker

Have you ever sat down to choose a menu item to make for dinner or a gathering and been overwhelmed? Well, I certainly have. We have over one hundred cookbooks in our house and the number grows almost weekly. We like books and we like to cook, so it's a natural hazard.

Then there are the hundreds of thousands of recipes online for each item, accessible by a few keystrokes. It might take you the rest of your life to filter through all the 'butternut squash soup' entries and by then, you and your now-skeletal fingers will not be interested in, or able to digest, food anymore.

Your television is bombarded with food and cooking shows, not to mention your social media feed with time-lapsed videos of unidentified hands making all sorts of delectable delights.

But do we really need to find a seventy-ninth way to garnish a basic hamburger with carefully sliced avocado and a fried egg? And how many times do we need to check our phones to monitor the number of likes we received for the photo of our latest baking creation, shot at the perfect angle?

My mother and her mother before her had one small box of recipes. Most were hand-written on cards that were heavily stained with a selection of the ingredients used therein on numerous previous attempts. There were even a few well-worn recipes snipped from the newspaper or a magazine, and a couple of tried and true coil-bound cookbooks with tattered pages.

And let's be clear – my mom and granny were no slouches in the kitchen, cooking for bridge club, knitting club, samba club, dinner parties and countless family get-togethers with awe-inspiring results every time. I still make some of those recipes and they will always be my favourites.

My purpose here is to suggest we all stop taking our cooking endeavours so seriously. Just like your hockey-loving son has only the most remote chance of making it to the National Hockey League – sorry – you and I will probably never be featured on the next network cooking challenge and win that trip to cook in France. Just saying.

10
Flight of Fear

Perhaps one of the most common areas of fear and anxiety in many people's lives corresponds to airline travel. And why not? When you boil it down to the most basic level, it involves packing a group of human beings into a metal tube and flinging them across the sky! Sorry – too basic?

As a young boy, I flew in tiny recreational aircraft with my father who had his private pilot's license. We flew all the way from Western Canada to the mid-western United States one summer and I got to be co-pilot. I have even been a passenger in a glider where they tow you into the sky with another plane and then let go and you fly around with no engine until you land! So at a young age, I could not say I had a fear of actually flying in an airplane.

Oddly enough, however, I developed a fear of flying later in life and could not rationally explain it, given my past history. I am talking about the kind of hyper-ventilating, palm-sweating, armrest-gripping type of fear as an airplane takes off, lands or makes funny noises in the air.

Through conversations with friends and colleagues, I eventually self-analyzed the fear to be related to the fact that I had a young family at home. Most of the occasions for my flying fear were on business trips where I was flying alone and was separated from my family. Somehow my mind had determined this made it a more fearful experience because if the plane went down and I perished, I would leave behind a family. As my family grew, the fear diminished.

Many people do have fears of flying in airplanes that cannot be easily explained away. If this applies to you or a loved one, I would encourage you to talk about it with people who fly often or members of an airline crew. They can put your mind at ease about the safety of airline travel (which we all know from statistics that it can be safer than driving in a car or even walking down the street).

There are many courses you can take to overcome this fear as well. Some of the major airlines even have clubs to assist and I have seen many photos of happy graduating classes boarding a flight.

11
Airport Anxiety

My current and persistent anxiety with airline travel centres around time. Getting to the airport on time, making your way through check-in, customs and security with enough time before the flight, the flight leaving on time and arriving on time!

If your anxiety is like mine, my advice is to give yourself time in order to combat the timing anxiety! Plan to arrive at the airport early so all those details can be carried out in a non-hurried fashion. And give yourself plenty of time for your trip to the airport – taking into account traffic, weather and unreliable taxis or public transit – so your time pre-flight is not rushed.

If you plan ahead to be very early to the airport, you can have some fun with this and even make it an important part of the trip. Our particular ritual involves not eating until we are all settled at the airport – mostly because eating when you are stressed and your stomach is doing flip-flops is not a great idea. But then we have a nice meal or a drink at the airport to start the trip off right.

Another thing you can do is to bring along your guidebooks, magazines and itineraries and spend a little time going over them and getting yourself all excited for what's to follow.

There is nothing worse than a delayed flight after you have managed your part of the time equation leading up to the flight. It's not that we can't be patient and wait a little longer, but it is all the thoughts about possible missed connections or cancelled reservations at the other end.

We recently took our family overseas for a Christmas vacation, leaving just a few days before Christmas, and our outgoing flight was delayed by four hours. Unfortunately four hours was the time we had allotted at the other end for a very important connection to another flight. It was important because it was just days before Christmas and every other flight was full!

And when your mind is in that mode of extreme anxiety, even the smallest of things, like the plastic 'joy' decoration in the airport restaurant, make you want to scream! I nearly did.

I needed my own advice in this case and should have allowed more time for the connection, perhaps even an overnight stay at the first destination, given the time of year. But we are all in a rush to get to the holiday destination, aren't we? If you can, slow it down and allow more time for the inevitable delays of busy airports.

Allowing time when you first arrive at your destination is important too. On this particular trip, we did not plan any activity for the first day in order to be able to recover from the many hours of travel and jet lag, and it was a wise decision. I have often heard it said to give yourself 'a day to get lost' at your destination with no plans. Great advice! Sometimes, those days turn out to the best part of the trip.

12
Get Away

With a partner who works for an airline, we tend to travel slightly more than the average couple, I would say. But that doesn't mean anxiety does not come along with us in our baggage from time to time. We just haven't allowed it to hold us back from some wonderful travels.

The evening news and your social media feed thrives off the old adage of: "If it bleeds, it leads." In a split second, you can be completely up to date on the latest terrorist attack or death-causing virus in a faraway land. The monsters are no longer hiding under your bed or in the dark forest; they are beamed onto your television and mobile devices for instant consumption.

Fear of the unknown is easy and powerful. It gets higher ratings and lots of 'likes'. Fear is what politicians and insurance companies count on to keep us voting and buying policies. So when the fear of travel takes over our brains, we tend to stay home, do nothing and hide. One of our American friends recently told us with complete confidence we would be mugged and murdered when we disembarked our cruise ship in Greece. I am here at my computer to assure you that did not happen.

My own truth, proven over and over again from travel, is the world is an awesome place to explore and find opportunity. Strangely enough, most of the people on the planet are doing the exact same thing as you – trying to make good lives for themselves and their families in safe and welcoming places. It has been our absolute pleasure to meet some of these people and be welcomed into their worlds. Many have become lifelong friends.

What should make you truly anxious is the thought of missing out on walking the hillside pathways of Cinque Terre in Italy with a giant pizza as your reward at the end of the trail, or dining on the back of a ship facing the lights of Monte Carlo as the million-dollar yachts arrive and depart around you. If we had let our own anxiety hold us back, we would have missed out on the sights, sounds, smells and tastes of Mexico, Spain, France, Italy, Greece, Malta and the United Kingdom – so far. That is what *really* scares me.

13
Sick and Tired

If you happen to get sick and normally go to school, work in an office or spend your day around other people, you should take your grandmother's advice and stay home. She was right when she told you to get plenty of rest and drink lots of fluids which maybe even included some chicken soup.

Unfortunately, taking a sick day can be another source of stress and anxiety for many of us! My long-time employer allows twelve paid sick days each year and I still feel an incredible amount of guilt if I take one. Silly? Yes.

Once again, this is a fear caused by a belief that being away from school or work will result in failure of some sort. Someone else could do your work and be better at it or you could miss that one morsel of knowledge that will never come your way again. Highly unlikely! One or two days away will not jeopardize anything and you will return as a better-rested person and hopefully without infecting others.

14
Cocktail Catastrophes

I do not like cocktail parties. I get extremely anxious trying to make small talk and I don't eat much because I worry that the food has been out for too long and is going to make me sick. What a mess I am!

This is not really a huge surprise since I know I am an introvert. Introverts get their energy from within and extroverts get theirs from others – and that is why those extroverts are usually the 'life of the party'.

I am not, however, a social misfit and neither are most introverts. I have learned that I thrive and enjoy social interaction in smaller groups. I enjoy a dinner party or appetizers with one or two other couples or coffee with a friend. And when we do have larger parties at our home or I am part of planning a big gathering, I prefer to be the one fussing behind the scenes to make sure everything is perfect rather than the one out front having all the stimulating conversations.

The trick here is to know what you're good at and avoid what you're not. We all have to endure social situations that we would rather skip. But getting out and seeing people is one of the best ways to overcome anxiety, so missing out is taking us in the wrong direction.

15
Fear of Falling

If you live in a place where snow and ice are not an issue, I congratulate you. Where I live in Canada, snow and ice are a big part of winter and that makes driving and walking quite hazardous. In just one year in my home province, falls on ice led to almost seventeen thousand trips to hospital emergency departments.

I have a big fear of falling and assume it is because I have seen it happen to so many people and the resulting broken hips, ribs, arms and legs. As you get older, this becomes a bigger fear because of the slower healing process and none of us wants to be in the hospital or away from our daily lives because of a silly accident.

It's not the fastest or most graceful way to walk, but have you ever seen a penguin slip? Their waddle works because of balance – low and slow is the key. So when the ground is covered in ice, prevent a fall by acting a bit like a penguin!

Bend slightly and walk flat-footed, pointing your feet out slightly like a penguin. Keep your centre of gravity over your feet as much as possible and watch where you are stepping! Take shorter, shuffle-like steps with your arms at your sides (not in your pockets!) and use them for balance. If you have to carry things, put them in a backpack or shoulder bag so your hands are free to help you if you fall. Like driving in bad conditions, the key is to go slowly.

Wear sturdy footwear with ankle support and good grips. Leave the suicide shoes, as I call them, with leather soles at home or bring them with you in a bag – you don't need to look pretty 100% of the time. You can even buy some great little contraptions called ice cleats that are basically rubber soles with metal grips that slip over your regular boots or footwear. These can be kept at the ready in your bag or in your car for when you find yourself needing to traverse a snowy or icy path.

The message here is we can all still get outside and enjoy some fresh air and sunshine even when the weather makes it look as though we can't. There is nothing better for one's mood than being in the outdoors and fear of falling is a sorry reason to stop us.

16
Your Brain on Drugs

Many years ago, there was a television commercial that was supposed to scare people away from taking illegal drugs. If my memory serves me correctly, it showed a frying pan with the line, "This is drugs," and then another photo of an egg frying in the pan with the line, "This is your brain on drugs." I'm not sure how effective it was, but it's interesting that I have remembered it after all these years!

Of course the 'drugs' to which they were referring at the time were things like marijuana, heroin, hash and LSD. And I am really the wrong person to pretend to have any knowledge of this because I was pretty much a goodie-two-shoes and never went near any of it!

But prescription drugs for me are another story. I could likely fill a page of this book with a list of all the medications I have taken at one time or another in my life. And I could fill another book with my thoughts on how the medical profession is trained to prescribe drugs before looking at root causes, natural solutions and nutrition. For much of my first marriage, our family doctor was what I would now refer to as a pusher.

Throughout that first marriage and that part of my life, I was not only extremely anxious, but also often depressed and suicidal. Of course in hindsight, it is easy to diagnose that I was a gay man living a straight life and since I hadn't quite figured that out, I was a little messed up! I was prescribed numerous anti-depressants which of course all had their own horrible side-effects. And for anyone who has been on an anti-depressant drug, they know the worst side-effect is the numbing of all your feelings – good and bad.

Side-effects of drugs are a whole science to themselves with some very scary outcomes. When I injured my lower back – and in the almost twelve months it took for a clear diagnosis of what I had actually done to myself – I was on so many pain medications that I needed a spreadsheet in order to keep track of them. About half the drugs were for the pain and to help me sleep through it and the other half were to assist with side-effects like constipation and stomach upset. I remember having another very complicated spreadsheet for when I came off the drugs before surgery, because many of the drugs were addicting and you cannot just take them one day and stop the next.

Most of my adult life, I have had high cholesterol and medical doctors have fancy 'equations' to determine if you need to be put on statin medication to improve your levels. I have taken dozens of statins in my life and did so until I did some research into the bad side-effects I was getting and stopped. With the help of my naturopathic doctor and a much-improved diet, I now keep my cholesterol in check with the food I eat and the exercise I get.

Near the time when I finally came out as gay and my first marriage ended, I was having obvious trouble 'performing' in the bedroom, shall we say, and was prescribed medication for erectile dysfunction. It seems ridiculous now to even be writing this! And despite being very expensive at the time, the drug did nothing for me or the situation, a great example of how a drug cannot fix what your mind has decided upon.

After the marriage ended and I had moved out of the house, I was given a cabinet full of new drugs for my ills, which included extreme anxiety, suicidal thoughts and the inability to sleep. When I met Les, who became my future spouse, however, all my anxiety disappeared and I slept like a baby without a single pill. Coincidence? Love as a sleeping pill. Love as the ultimate anti-depressant. I highly recommend it.

17
Superstition Ain't the Way

It's odd the way songs stay in your head. And even odder is how you can hear an old song and be transported back to the exact time and place where you heard it or listened to it a lot. I think it maybe was more prominent back in my younger days when songs were only available live, on the radio or on your home stereo system and not instantly accessible online, with your phone or mp3 player. But I digress.

On our family's trip to Hawaii for Christmas in 1972, Stevie Wonder's *Superstition* was a top song on the radio, playing loudly as we bopped around the island in our snazzy convertible. And every time I hear that song, it brings me back to that vacation.

The lyrics of the song highlight a challenge that many of us have, however, which is a fear of superstitious things like walking under a ladder, a broken mirror and the number 13. As Stevie sings, "When you believe in things you don't understand, then you suffer. Superstition ain't the way."

Another thing that has fortunately almost disappeared is the chain letter. Oh, how I disliked those things! Back in the snail-mail days, you would receive a letter in the mail that stated if you did not send it on to 'X' number of family and friends in a certain number of days, horrible things would happen to you. More recently, I have seen similar things on social media and you have instant regret when you click on a post that asks you to share it or face all kinds of evil if you do not!

I will admit to being afraid of all those things in my life. Perhaps 'afraid' is the wrong word, but I think many of us are conscious of the threat of something bad happening when we walk under a ladder or a black cat crosses our path. As I have written before in these pages, fear is an emotion that comes from a belief that something is dangerous or likely to cause pain or grief. We fear the outcome of things and events we don't even know will ever happen simply because our minds are hard-wired to, especially if you have heard all these superstitions over and over again and believe that not forwarding a chain letter or post will be detrimental.

So all we need to do is move our minds into a place of happiness and security when these situations arise. Sounds easy, right?

Start to think of the number 13 as your lucky number. Walk boldly under a ladder if it is the only way through, as long as you have made sure it is safe to do so. Make sure that little kitten has made it safe to the other side of the road, rather than fearing the meaning of the whole thing. And if you break a looking glass, for goodness sake, clean it up quickly before someone gets a shard of glass in their foot. That's the only bad luck that will come.

18
Reading the Post

It's interesting how words can change meaning over many years, or how some words never really existed before. Our Italian language teacher was recently telling us how since the words 'computer' and 'internet' did not exist before, there is no Italian word for them. The words for computer and internet in Italian are therefore 'computer' and 'internet'. Ta-da!

Another concept or word that has drastically changed is the concept of posting something. It used to mean you placed something in the mail for the post office to deliver – and, of course, still means that. But primarily, we hear about 'posting' to our social media channels in order to instantaneously inform the world about our moods, activities or what we made for dinner.

As a kid, my sisters and I also posted things on our bedroom walls. The goal, it seemed, was to cover every bit of exposed wall with posters. Almost every store had a poster section and I remember even being able to order posters through a mail order service at school. Big business!

And just like our social media sites, the posters you put up on your walls spoke volumes about who you were. My sister had lots of posters of rock bands and peace symbols because that was her passion at the time. My walls were slightly different.

I am not sure how many young boys would have posters on their walls that said things like, "When life gives you lemons, make lemonade," and "I know you think you understand what you thought I said, but I'm not sure you realize that what you heard is not what I meant." I am not making this stuff up!

I also had a couple of posters with race cars on them, because I thought this was what a young boy should have. Let's be clear, I did not like race cars. I had the posters up to make it look like I was interested in normal boy stuff.

Past generations had their own social media and we still have these traditions, although there are no devices required. A flag at half-mast for Remembrance Day shows others your respect for the fallen heroes of past wars. People put coloured lights on their houses at Christmas and carved pumpkins on their door steps at Halloween and then the neighbours, family and friends who come to visit, and those who pass by, see the 'posts' and tell others if they 'like' it or don't.

So although the way we post has changed a bit over the years, my message here is to pay attention to what you put out there and also to look at what your friends and loved ones put up. It's a great little window into our moods and might help you better understand yourself and others.

19
Pee Pain

Yes, I am really going there. At this point in my life and in this book, nothing is sacred. So we might as well talk about the fear and anxiety caused by the use of public washrooms. First of all, this fear is much more common than you might think.

I will put my hand in the air as having had this challenge as long as I can remember. I have found some tips and tricks along the way, but it has never really gone away. And since going to the bathroom is a basic human need, it can be quite frustrating.

It doesn't help that most public washrooms for men were designed by some kind of cave man. For the female readers, this may come as news, since a comical chat around the office cooler recently revealed that most ladies do not really understand how it 'works' in a men's washroom. Let me enlighten you.

Unless you are in a very high-end establishment, men's washrooms usually have a long wall of urinals placed side by side with no barriers. In some cases, there are not even individual urinals but instead a large trough-like apparatus that everyone shares. So out comes the part and you do your number-one business for all to see.

One of the large movie theatres in our city does have barriers between the urinals, but the well-meaning designer used a very glossy tile on the wall, which acts as a mirror so you can see everything down the whole line. Really?

There's even some unwritten protocol about this whole procedure. If someone is already there, you never choose the spot immediately next to them. If more than one person is already there, you have to make a careful choice about exactly where to stand. I remember a video game a few years back that let you play out these scenarios and get points for the correct choices. It was hilarious!

Of course, just like a women's washroom, you can always choose a normal stall with a proper toilet, but those are usually very scarce in the men's room and there is usually a line up. And in whichever washroom you might find yourself, a line-up of people waiting does nothing to help the anxiety of performing quickly.

For what it's worth, I know this anxiety is not limited to men. Having to do one's private business sitting inches away from someone else with only a thin barrier between you is just not natural in my opinion, although it always gives you the opportunity to critique people's socks and shoe choices.

This is where the bit of advice comes in. I have found that the best way to overcome this anxiety is to make a bit of a game of it. Or at least take your mind off the immediate situation.

If you are a bathroom reader like me, take a book or magazine with you. Our wonderful little handheld devices have allowed us to almost always have something to 'read' in our pockets or bags. Just don't drop it in the toilet or you will have a whole new thing to be anxious about!

If you are not so well equipped or are in a serious rush to complete the task, I have found some success in focusing on something in the room or singing myself a little tune. Sing to yourself, not out loud. In other words, take your mind off the reality of where you are and what has to be done.

20
Dining Dashingly

One of my favourite things to do is to dine out at a restaurant. I absolutely love it, whether it is by myself because no one else is around, with my partner for date night and when we travel or with friends and family.

I think I come by this quite naturally, as my mom loved to eat out. She always said that because she lived through the Great Depression, it was her reward to eat at nice restaurants. And so we did.

Mom was quite devious about this sometimes in order to get my father to agree. "I haven't taken anything out," or "Everything is frozen," were quite common excuses she would use. I certainly didn't argue and was fortunate to try a lot of restaurants at a young age.

But somewhere along the way, I managed to develop an anxiety associated with dining out that can be quite frustrating. And since it all revolves around money, it was likely started when I first became the one responsible for paying the bill!

When I am handed a menu, my eyes first go to the prices and then to the descriptions. Les and I are the same in this regard, so we are not a good pair when we are both trying to pick the lowest priced thing on the menu. Of course this is extremely unfortunate since some higher priced items may be the specialty of the establishment and the whole reason we are visiting.

So along the way, I have developed some tricks to help me reduce this anxiety and enjoy the whole experience much more. After all, if you have decided you can afford to eat out, you may as well enjoy it!

Most restaurants have their menus posted online these days, so a little advance research can help a great deal. If the prices really are too high for your budget, select a different restaurant. If not, you can look at all the options and decide in advance what will please your palette and your wallet at the same time.

Another thing we really like to do is to ask the server for their recommendations. This way, you not only get to try something that is someone else's favourite, but it takes the pressure off your decision. And I have found that in most cases, the server does not recommend the most expensive items anyway.

One of the other benefits of eating healthy and controlling portion size is that most restaurant portions are quite large and you will have some food left to take home with you. That way, you get an extra meal out of the deal!

21
Read the Signs

When my best friend, Kelly, and I lived in the same city many years ago, she had a habit of ending our telephone conversations with the phrase, "I'll call you later." The trouble with that, for me, was that I was very distraught when she did *not* call me later.

Around the same time, my first boyfriend, after I had come out as gay, would use the same line. And when he didn't call me later, I was sent into a spiral of despair. I was going through a very difficult time in my life and I clearly took everything literally.

It seems pretty obvious now and as I write these words that both people were merely using what we call a figure of speech. They meant, of course, that we would speak again at some future time – yet undetermined, not later this hour, today or even this week, necessarily.

There is a comedian that uses examples like this as part of his material and one that always makes me howl with laughter is the one about the party-pooper. Someone tells him that another person is a party-pooper (meaning they take all the joy out of something fun), but he thinks they mean a person that actually poops at parties. It's hilarious. But I digress.

My purpose here is to highlight how many of the things our friends, family and coworkers might say to us need to be put through a filter and, to use another figure of speech, taken with a grain of salt. And when we are anxious about a relationship, it seems to make things worse.

This can take a bit of practice, but is really helpful in relieving anxiety about very minor things. It might even help you to keep a journal. If you write down that your friend has said, "Let's get together for coffee," exactly twenty-six times in the last three months, it might mean that she wants *you* to make the arrangements – or it is just her way of saying you need to spend more time together and she is not sure how to make that happen. It helps to look on the positive side that your friend isn't saying, "Have a nice life!"

The important thing in all cases is for you to stop worrying about what it all means and either accept it as the person's go-to phrase or take some action. Call *them* later. Arrange a coffee date soon. Or even tell them it's annoying you.

22
Get Your Poop in a Group

For sure, we know this book has reached rock bottom when we get to the chapter about poop. And since we have already covered the use of public washrooms elsewhere, it kind of seems natural. Actually there is nothing more natural!

Believe it or not, people do have anxiety over this very subject. A lot of people cannot go, do not go often enough, go too much or it hurts when they go. It is called a bowel movement for a reason – food and toxins need to move through your body and find their way out. And if things are not moving well, it's problematic.

Let's get even more graphic. I consider your toilet the perfect indicator of your digestive health. If you've heard the phrase, 'making a call on the porcelain phone', then think of it as an app that tells you if you're healthy.

The goal is to have something well-formed. Some say it should form an 'S' shape in the bowl. And then there's the colour. The goldilocks principle applies here since you want something not too dark and not too light. But I'm getting ahead of myself.

If we know what the end goal is, how do we get there? Obviously what comes out is a product of what you put in. If you're eating highly processed foods and very few fresh vegetables, you may get something that is not ideal at the other end too. Everyone knows what happens to corn – it basically comes out exactly as it went in because there is little or no nutritional value in it.

After many years of less-than-perfect results, I now know what works for me. So let me share. It's all about water and movement.

When you get up in the morning, whatever time that is, drink at least five hundred millilitres and preferably one litre of fresh, filtered water. Room temperature water is easier to drink and less shocking on your warm, freshly-awakened body. I have that water ready for me the night before, so there is no barrier or excuse to prevent this from happening.

The next thing is to get your body moving. My personal thing is not an all-out workout in the morning, but maybe it is yours. What I do is some very gentle stretches and twists and I actually do them right in the shower.

And guess what happens moments after I emerge from the shower? You guessed it – I hope – a perfect and effortless event on the toilet. And as for that 'poop app' to which I referred, I can tell instantly if I ate something that did not agree with me and can adjust my selections in the future.

23
Seasons

Ah yes, the seasons. I wonder how many poems and songs have been written about the wonders of winter, spring, summer and fall? And how many theories might there be about the way they can affect our moods and feelings?

Where I live in Canada, we get four pretty distinctive seasons and sometimes all in one day! Our winters are cold and snowy, spring is short, summer is warm and fall may or not show up at all if we get an early winter. But it's the amount of sun that can really mess with a lot of people and I am included in that crowd.

Most of us feel a little sad when the warm days of summer are replaced with cooler mornings and evenings. And if you go to school or work at a regular time each day, you soon see the sun rising later and going down sooner.

Some people are so affected by this that they are diagnosed with something called Seasonal Affective Disorder, which carries the very appropriate acronym SAD. For those with extreme cases, it can be debilitating.

Symptoms that are common with SAD include fatigue, irritability, joint or muscle pain, sleep difficulties and loss or gain of weight and appetite. In general, feelings of hopelessness, feeling deflated or disheartened and withdrawal from normal activities are what people express.

My friend Kelly and I will usually have a telephone call in early fall each year where we talk about the 'funk' we are in. It can be very hard to describe to others, but we both get it. Some people call it just feeling 'down'.

As I said, most of us feel at least a little different with the change of seasons, even if we do not have an extreme case. And there are a few things I have tried that can help.

Since I am a total geek when it comes to spreadsheets and charts, I have developed a little clock to track the seasons. And funny enough, I have never actually drawn the clock on a piece of paper. There are a few versions floating around, but I have never seen one quite like mine. I can see it quite clearly in my head since it mimics a normal twelve-hour clock.

My 'clock' is divided into fifty-two weeks instead of sixty minutes. June 21st or Summer Solstice is at the twelve o'clock position at the top. That's my favourite day of the year! It has the longest day and most amount of sun, unless it's raining, of course. At the bottom or six o'clock position is Winter Solstice or December 21st.

That leaves Fall Equinox or September 21st at the three o'clock position and Spring Equinox at nine o'clock. So you get four equal quarters with thirteen weeks each.

So call me a clock-watcher or whatever you like, but I find this somehow soothing to be able to picture where a given day is on the chart. As I write these words, it is the end of January and we are about six weeks past Winter Solstice. I am not a fan of January, in general, but this allows me to play the game that if we are six weeks past the darkest day of the year, therefore we have also passed the darkest twelve weeks of the year that lie at the bottom of my clock. And that's roughly the darkest one-quarter of the year! Are you following me?

What I always find interesting is that I seldom use the clock – or picture it in my mind – when the sun is rising early and staying up late. No need to count away those days. And since the fall is usually busy with new activities and preparations for the Christmas season, I don't really focus on those times either.

The bottom line for the time of year that affects you most – for me the bottom half of my clock – is to find ways to overcome your negative symptoms. Get outside as much as you can, even if you have to bundle up. Put your face to the sun and practise reviewing your gratitude list. If you can't get outside, sit in a sunny window with some pillows and blankets, a candle burning, your favourite book and a cup of something warm in your hands.

If you have an indoor hobby, fall and winter are obviously the best times to hone to this skill and maybe even develop a new one. And for those of us in colder climates, this is of course also the best time to plan oneself a vacation to a sunny and warm spot!

In the coldest and darkest time of the year, the brightest fruit is in season—citrus! Oranges, grapefruits, lemons, and limes are at their peak, so take advantage of it by munching on one or making some of your favourite citrus recipes. Just like the sun, for some reason bright orange and yellow fruits and vegetables are instant mood-enhancers.

For my dearly departed mother's 70th birthday many years ago, we gave her a large garden rock with the words "No winter lasts forever; no spring skips its turn" inscribed on it. This is worth keeping in mind too.

24
On the Job

I wonder if our ancestors, or even our great-grandparents, had the kind of anxiety we have about what we do to make a living? Our jobs or professions, bringing home the bacon, whatever you call it. I am guessing they did not.

Our hunter-gatherer ancestors really only had a few things to worry about, finding enough food for survival, having a place to live and stay warm and protecting themselves from human and animal enemies. I'm certainly not saying that having to hunt for food or run away from sabre-tooth tigers was easy, but somehow I think they spent no time stressing out about it all.

I've read some documentation that suggests the average hunter-gatherer spent about twenty hours a week doing the stuff I just mentioned. And they spent the rest of their time just hanging out with their tribe of family and friends, not quite the fifty-to-sixty hours per week the average adult spends at – and getting to and from – their job these days.

I'm not sure I had as much anxiety about my job when I was younger as I do now, but it pains me to see my twenty-something daughters already having anxiety about their work lives. Do I have the right job? Why don't I get paid more? I'm pretty wonderful, after all? Do I really have to do this for forty more years? Why can't I just work from home?

What is also interesting is how their anxiety differs from mine. Just like mine differs from what my parents or grandparents might have felt.

The place where I work is pretty stable and not as prone to the ups and downs of the economy as some industries. But about ten years ago, they did a major restructuring in order to streamline and cut costs, and thirty of my colleagues lost their jobs overnight. I have never really gotten over that. And so, even though I perform very well at my work, somehow it just got into my core and has caused me to fear losing my job ever since.

This kind of anxiety can be absolute reality in many workplaces of the 21st century. The world is just moving too fast and so much new technology is being introduced that it cannot possibly avoid resulting in loss of jobs.

Some of us, like me, carry our stress in our bodies too. When I moved to a different office environment and began reporting to a new boss several years ago, I developed a permanently stiff neck. I thought it was my chair, the position of my desk or the angle of my computer and spent countless hours adjusting everything to try and get it right. I was somehow oblivious to the fact the environment itself was stressing me out!

My office has a pretty strict dress code as well, which in itself can cause daily stress as you stand before the mirror just before walking out the door. Ladies must wear panty hose except in July and August, something I have never worn but about which I am told are complete torture. Gentlemen are supposed to wear jackets and ties, the latter I consider to be the worst invention known to mankind.

But despite my anxiety, I have never been called out on my wardrobe in twenty-three years of employment. I wonder why I worry, but sometimes it doesn't seem to stop me.

In a case like the dress code, it helps to examine the facts, make a decision and move on. I am following the documented dress code. I always look neat and professional and nobody has ever said I do not. Time for me to move on.

25
The Imposter

While we are on the topic of stress in the workplace, I have another doozy that I suspect a few people share with me, or at least I *hope* I am not the only one!

I wrote earlier in these pages about how I feared I was mentally challenged as a young boy and this type of fear has carried into my adult life in a slightly different way. Sometimes, as I sit in a meeting or am receiving recognition for a job well done, I feel like an imposter. I feel like I am really not qualified to do the task for which I have been assigned, but fortunately everyone has been fooled by my ingenious disguise.

Sometimes this type of fear can enter our personal lives too. Many parents go through this anxiety of thinking they are still kids themselves and how they could not possibly be qualified to raise one.

If your mind tortures you with what-if and catastrophic thoughts about your ability to do your job, raise your kids or perform normal tasks, you are not alone. We need to focus on healing our relationship with ourselves to get past this.

It is hard for us to get to know ourselves. It is not something that is taught in school or passed down from other generations. It is normal for us, especially as children, to feel overwhelmed by painful events such as I did by being bullied. Experiences of feeling unloved and powerless become beliefs over time. These false core beliefs of unworthiness drive our thoughts and actions.

I was raised in a household with very strict rules. So if you're like me, you may hide out by being good. I have often told the story of how, as the youngest of three children, I felt I had to be good in order to make up for the crazy things my two older sisters did. But in reality, I did a lot of stupid things myself as rebellion for being the *good* child.

Hiding out may work okay for a short time and in our younger days, but it is not very effective at building relationships with others in our personal or business lives. Later in this book, I go into some strategies for getting to know ourselves better and releasing some of these old learned patterns that are no longer serving us. We all deserve – and need – to be our authentic selves.

26
Money-Makers

Few subjects in the anxiety department can stack up against worrying about money and our finances. And while we all know the adage that money doesn't bring happiness, I think we can all agree a certain amount of it is necessary in our modern world in order to survive.

As young people, we are directed and encouraged to study hard at school for basically one reason: so we can get to a future graduation day and move on to a job or more school. It may sound simplistic, but beyond learning to read and write, that is really the only goal and it hasn't changed much in the last hundred years. We learn so we can earn.

So, very often, the degree to which we succeed or fail in school predicts our income-earning potential for most of our lives. This sets us up for anxiety from the very beginning, since we start to compare the amount of money we have to others and, like hamsters on an exercise wheel, we can never really reach the imaginary goal of *enough*.

Along my journey, I have found a few things that can mitigate the anxiety about money and how much of it we have. In my first book, I wrote about how my mom was the keeper of the financial records in our home. Although she did not work outside our home after my sisters and I were born, she kept the family earnings on track and I always felt we lived very well despite being a one-income family.

Mom had a giant ledger with green paper like an old-school accountant and she entered every expense in detail. When I was old enough to have my first part-time job, I mirrored this practice with my own little ledger book. I have done this my whole life and now use a spreadsheet on my computer, but the process is the same.

By keeping track of your income and expenses, you start to see patterns that you are either pleased with or not. If you are spending too much in one area, you can clearly see it and make alterations. Good records also ensure you never miss a bill payment, which can be the quickest way to a bad credit rating and a lifetime of paying more than you should when it comes time to borrow for a car or home.

One of the other uses of financial record-keeping is to set goals. I saved for my first house by dividing each pay into actual envelopes for rent, groceries, clothing, entertainment and house savings. I never borrowed from the house envelope and was able to save enough in one year for the down payment.

The other side of this equation is to determine your *real* hourly wage – and I do mean the real one. Since any job, profession or business is all about trading hours for dollars, it's a great place to start to get some clarity on our situation.

We can all figure out our real hourly income even though we might be paid monthly or every second week. So let's say you make $25 per hour. But do you really? If you spend two or four extra hours each day getting ready for work and getting yourself to and from work, you need to add those hours in as well. That might take your wage down to $16 if it's really sixty hours a week you dedicate to your job.

Do you buy a coffee, latte, lunch or snacks during your work day that you might not buy if you were at home? Best is to add this in too – or rather deduct it from your pay. And many parents have childcare or pet-care expenses that are a necessity when they are elsewhere on the job. How about the special wardrobe you might need?

I hope you can see where I am going with this! Once you take the time to calculate what your *real* income is, you can then use it to make some of your purchasing decisions. If you have it calculated to $10 per hour and an item you want to buy costs $500, you can quite quickly decide if the item is worth fifty hours of your time. This can extend to major purchases like rent, a mortgage or a new car and perhaps help you steer away from over-extending yourself.

My other piece of advice is much more philosophical, but it does have merit. If we are what we eat, as they say, then we are also what we think about. And if you are constantly thinking about the money you do not have and the bills you do have, you can guess the result – less money and more bills.

If you have taken the time to do some tracking and calculations, you should know exactly how much money you have at your disposal and the need to worry about what you do not have disappears. And as always, practising gratitude for what we have is also a great way to reduce anxiety.

27
Over Puts You Under

I was always taught to be really good at something and I have discovered I am really good at overthinking. I wonder if I misunderstood this lesson. Overthinking is the art of creating problems that aren't even there in the first place. And I do my best fretting at about 2:00 a.m. in the morning.

Over-thinkers like me rehash conversations from the day before, second-guess decisions and imagine horrible outcomes for the future. Sometimes it is like watching a taped version of my meetings that have already occurred and a preview of the ones coming up. Some people stretch this out much further in both directions, worrying about things they did as a child or what will happen to them as an elderly person.

The challenge with these thought patterns is not the thinking itself. After all, thinking is good as it helps us make good decisions and learn from mistakes. But if you have *analysis paralysis*, as I like to call it, you cannot move forward and get things done. Overthinking almost always leads us down the 'cons' side of the pros and cons list and focuses on negative things.

After years of professional worrying, I have discovered a few patterns and therefore a few ways to overcome my ruminating. My middle-of-the-night sessions usually occur when I have had an exceptionally busy day and have fallen into bed exhausted and without time for reflection. It's not surprising then that my brain wakes me up halfway through the night to decompress. I have a much more restful sleep if I have incorporated some thinking time into my evening schedule and have already reviewed everything before my head hits the pillow.

It also helps to be a bit of detective and lawyer when negative thoughts start to crowd your mind. Do a bit of interrogation and cross-examination on yourself to see if there is any evidence to prove that the outcome you are envisioning can actually occur. Will you really be fired for making a silly comment in that meeting? Are you really going to be living on the streets because you didn't save enough money for retirement?

In his famous book *How to Stop Worrying and Start Living*, Dale Carnegie shared a story from Reverend William Wood in which he talks about how washing dishes with his wife helped him stop his mind from worrying. He said the reason they didn't mind washing the dishes was because they were only washing one day's dishes at a time. If they had looked ahead when they first got married at all the dishes they would have to wash in their marriage, the pile of dirty dishes in their minds would have been 'bigger than a barn'. As soon as he realized his overthinking was like trying to wash today's dishes and yesterday's dishes and dishes that weren't even dirty yet, he realized how ridiculous it was.

It might help if we all learned to only focus on today's dishes, meetings, relationships and what we are having for dinner.

The Pills
Those Things We Can Change

28
Just Breathe

What could be more natural than breathing? Our bodies do it every minute from birth to death, so I'm guessing it is pretty important!

Unfortunately, we don't really need to think about breathing – it's unconscious – and so it lacks importance in our busy lives. But when you are feeling anxious or fearful, there is nothing better to help your body than some *conscious* breathing.

Most of us take very shallow breaths from the top part of our chest or maybe even from the shoulders up. And sometimes if we are in a really bad situation or in physical or mental pain, we hold our breath! And that's one of the worst things you can do because it stops sending oxygen to your brain and other cells.

Have you ever had a massage or physiotherapy and when the practitioner hits a sore spot, you tense your muscles and hold your breath? If you have, the therapist has likely reminded you to breathe deeply or 'breathe through the pain'.

Like many things, breath work can be learned in countless books, videos and courses, but I encourage you to keep it simple. Find three to five minutes in your day to stop and do some purposeful deep breathing. It doesn't even matter if the air goes in your nose and out your mouth or any combination thereof! You can be sitting, standing or lying down. Whatever works for you is just fine.

Take a big breath in and feel it fill your whole chest and body – hold it for a few seconds and release the air. Repeat this 3-4 times and take a break. Then do it all over again. As I said, a total of three to five minutes does the trick.

The benefit to our bodies is this delivers oxygen to our cells, including the brain. You might even feel a little light-headed and have a tingly sensation afterwards. It also activates our immune system which can often sit dormant. But most of all, it takes you away from your fears and stresses for a few moments and recharges your body. It's really difficult to think about whatever is bothering you when you are thinking about your breath going in and out.

29
Water the Crops

I need to take more seriously my own advice when it comes to water. It is so good for you. The average adult should be drinking at least eight glasses a day. Organizations like Weight Watchers teach this before you even walk in the door.

Without proper hydration, your body gets tired and wrinkled and holds onto water like it will never see another drop. Just look at me! Most of us need to drink a lot more water.

Scientists say our bodies are made up of 70 percent salty water. Overnight, while we are sleeping, we become dehydrated and need to replenish our water resources right away upon rising. And I already talked about how drinking water as the first thing you do in the morning helps your body do its pooping business!

The one trick I have adopted that works well is to have water handy at all times. I have filtered water ready in my bathroom so I can drink at least five hundred millilitres as soon as I wake up in the morning. This gets your metabolism going and kick-starts your day.

I have a water bottle in my office that I can fill up at the office cooler to keep within arm's reach as I work. If it's in front of me, I drink it. I drink water at restaurants if it is put in front of me, yet forget to ask for it if it is not. If you are at all concerned that you might overeat at a party or restaurant, try drinking a glass of water before you get started – it works like a charm.

The bottom line is to make it simple for yourself and drink water. Your body will thank you.

30
Gratitude Is Good

We're all very familiar with gratitude. We practise it at Thanksgiving dinner when we *give thanks* for the bounty of the harvest and the food in front of us. Some of us might even do this before every meal. One of the first things our parents teach us is to say 'thank you' when someone gives us something or does a nice thing.

If we are truly able to cultivate an attitude of gratefulness, however, it can take our mind and body to a better place – away from anxiety and fear of what we don't have or haven't yet achieved. It's a proven fact we have all experienced – a positive change in attitude improves our feelings and our behaviour. And if we have improved behaviours, it helps every aspect of our lives from our jobs to our love life!

To get good at gratitude, I encourage you to actually lower your gratitude level rather than raise it. There is nothing wrong with looking up at the skies and thanking our Creator for the universe, but I am talking about much smaller things here. Bear with me.

It's quite easy to be grateful for your loving partner, your wonderful children, a beautiful home or your successful career. And quite often, we only have gratitude for these things after they are impaired or taken away from us. What I am suggesting here is to take gratefulness down to a much more basic level.

Les and I recently bought some new sheets for our bed after fighting for months with low-quality ones that didn't stay in place on the mattress. We absolutely love the new sheets and I am grateful for them. I am grateful for them every time I get into bed!

Maybe your partner makes a fantastic cup of coffee that you have not been able to duplicate or you get that great coffee from the same smiling barista every morning. I don't partake in smoking, but maybe you enjoy a fine cigar, Friday nights with friends, your exercise routine or a crossword puzzle on Sunday morning – it's easy to be grateful for any one or all of these things. How about the hair on your head!

Many cultures are much better at gratitude than we North Americans. They are grateful for the sun that is shining, but equally grateful for the rain that falls as it brings nourishment to the land. Or they might be grateful they caught a fish because that means their family eats dinner tonight.

Despite it being one of the hardest, gut-wrenching things I have ever done in my entire life, I am grateful for having the courage to come out as gay. And that gratefulness is repeated every day. It gave me the courage to reach out to a sister from which I had been alienated for many years and we now have a close relationship. I was able to seek out and meet my wonderful life partner, Les. I no longer have to hide my true identity and personality behind a façade. I could go on for pages.

Once you have mastered the art of listing, and being thankful for, the countless little things in your life that make you happy, you can absolutely move on to the big, lumpy bits. This is where I find keeping a journal can be very beneficial.

Be thankful for your health, your wealth, your work, your hobbies, your wisdom and especially the love you share with family and friends. I can almost guarantee that your worries about what you *don't* have will slip away when you focus on all the wonderful things you *do* have.

31
Know Your ABCs

'In sickness and in health' has been part of traditional marriage vows in various religions for a very long time. So it stands to reason that being healthy is a big part of our lives if it requires being mentioned at your wedding!

Many of us have a fear of being unhealthy and getting sick. Why else do we worry about our weight and fund the billion-dollar weight-loss industry? Why do we schedule annual check-ups with our doctors when we feel perfectly fine? Why do we rush out to get flu shots every autumn?

Besides being uncomfortable and annoying, being sick takes us away from our regular lives, our families, our sources of income and makes life less enjoyable. And for someone as frugal as me, I hate that it costs money to buy medicine and remedies!

Whole books, movies and television shows are dedicated to being healthy and I could not possibly attempt to cover this subject adequately in one chapter. I do, however, know what works for me and the result is that I am seldom sick.

I take vitamins daily. There are two sides to this subject and many people and their doctors believe that supplementing vitamins is unnecessary if we eat a balanced diet. But guess what? Most of us do not eat a balanced diet and even if we do, the food of the 21st century is lacking in many nutrients.

Where I live in Canada, we have one of the highest rates of Multiple Sclerosis and it has been attributed to a lack of vitamin D since we stay inside so much in the winter and do not get much sun. So I take vitamin D.

Vitamin C has been shown to combat the common cold and also reduce the risk of some cancers. So I take vitamin C – and a lot of it in the winter when it is cold and flu season.

I take vitamin E for my skin and selenium for brain functioning and memory. I take coenzyme Q10 for heart health and cranberry for my prostate.

The truth is you cannot possibly overdose on vitamins. Our bodies will just poop and pee out what they do not need. I prefer to put them in there and let my body decide what it needs.

32
Food

While we are on the subject of being healthy, we should talk about what else goes in your mouth besides the vitamin supplements. Again, I know that there is a whole industry behind this, but many of us worry if we are getting the right information. And the advice seems to change almost daily about what is good and what is bad!

We have often heard the phrase, "You are what you eat." But you also feel what you eat. Foods create moods. And your doctor will rarely tell you this because many are just not trained in nutrition and would rather diagnose an ailment and prescribe a drug.

I prefer to take a really simple approach to eating and look at what worked for our parents, grandparents and ancestors. Human beings are hunter-gatherers and thrive on a plant-based diet and natural animal products. Our predecessors ate only what they could grow or gather nearby and the animals they could raise or hunt and eat in a very limited amount of time due to lack of storage.

There was no such thing as fast food or a frozen burrito with a long list of unpronounceable ingredients. It is no surprise that many of the ills facing us in our modern world can be linked to the crazy things being added to our food. Manufacturers process food in a way that strips nutrients, adds preservatives and pours in artificial *everything* to increase flavour and shelf life.

So while our anxiety about what to eat or what diet to follow can be overwhelming at times, it can be made quite easy by choosing things with no ingredient list at all. Every fresh piece of fruit, vegetable and meat stands alone with just one ingredient and there is no advanced science degree required to decipher the contents.

I have often heard we should be shopping the outside perimeter of a grocery store and never entering the aisles in the middle. Although your own grocery store or market may not be oriented this way, where I live, most food stores have the fresh produce, meat and bread around the outside and aisles of packaged or frozen food in the middle.

To take just one example of an under-appreciated food, let's talk about sweet potatoes. Most of us grew up only ever seeing this vegetable on the holiday table at Thanksgiving or Christmas, and then usually covered with sugar and nuts to make it an almost dessert-like offering.

But hiding behind those often dishevelled skins in the back corner of the grocery store, sweet potatoes rank the highest in nutritional value of all vegetables, almost double than that of the common potato. Their unique root storage proteins have fantastic antioxidant properties and they are an excellent source of vitamins A, C and B6, as well as manganese, potassium, iron, copper and dietary fibre. Even the bugs haven't caught on to sweet potatoes, since they also grow well in a variety of conditions without pesticides!

Les and I have sweet potatoes in the pantry at almost all times and have developed a triplet of super easy ways to enjoy them.

Spicy Sweet Potato 'Fries'!

They're not fried, but that's the way most people think of sweet potatoes that look like this on their plate. This is so easy and you can experiment with your own blend of spices to get a taste you enjoy or to change it up meal after meal. The salt and pepper are required, but everything else is up to you.

You will quickly note with most of the recipes I share in this book that I am a one-pot kind of guy. If I can modify a recipe to use fewer dishes, I will. I'm not lazy. Just efficient!

1-2 large or 3-4 small sweet potatoes
2 tablespoons olive oil
2 tablespoons melted butter, allowed to cool slightly
½ teaspoon coarse salt
1 teaspoon freshly ground black pepper
1 tablespoon paprika
½ teaspoon dried oregano
½ teaspoon dried thyme
½ teaspoon dried rosemary
½ teaspoon garlic powder
¼ teaspoon cayenne pepper

Alternate:

Omit all above spices (except salt and pepper) and substitute with 4 teaspoons curry powder.

Preheat oven to 375 degrees, adjusting oven rack to middle or slightly closer to bottom if it's a toss-up. Wash the sweet potatoes and cut into whatever shapes you desire – the key is make sure to get them all the same size so they cook at the same speed. You can cut them into 'fry' shapes or wedges or whatever your heart desires! Just don't make them too small or they will overcook.

Spread your cut creations out on a baking sheet or large baking dish. Drizzle the olive oil and butter over the sweet potatoes and then sprinkle on the salt, pepper and other spices. Now get your hands in there – I have found the best way to get everything evenly coated is to hand-toss. Use latex gloves if you wish!

Bake for 40 minutes without turning or peeking. Here's where the controversy comes in – most recipes tell you to turn them halfway, but I have found this is way too fiddly and breaks up your lovely creations before they have had a chance to get crispy. It also allows them to cool off!

Serve them hot and, if you have spiced them correctly, there is no need for sugar-laden ketchup (but mustard is okay).

Easy Sweet Potato Soup

It's easy because of the very few ingredients and delicious result, but you will need a blender or food processor – sorry.

4 tablespoons butter
1 onion, sliced thin
4 sprigs fresh thyme
4¼ cups water
2 pounds sweet potatoes
1 tablespoon brown sugar (coconut palm sugar is better)
½ teaspoon cider vinegar
Salt and pepper

Peel the sweet potatoes, keeping about one-quarter of the peels. Cut the potatoes in half lengthwise and then slice them about ¼ inches thick.

Melt the butter in a large pot over medium-low heat. Add the onion and thyme and cook until the onion is softened, but not yet browned. Add the water and increase the heat to high until it starts to boil. Remove the pot from the heat and add the sweet potatoes and reserved peels. Let this stand for 20 minutes, uncovered.

Add the sugar, vinegar, 1½ teaspoons salt and ¼ teaspoon pepper to the pot. Bring to a boil over high heat and then reduce to a gentle simmer, covering the pot and cooking until the potatoes are very soft (for about 15 minutes).

Discard the thyme sprigs and, working in batches, process the soup in a blender until smooth. Return the soup to a clean pot and bring it back to a simmer, adding a bit more salt and pepper if you think it needs it. You may also need to add a little more water to get the soup to the consistency you like.

For a special dinner party, drizzle a little plain yoghurt over the top of each bowl or add some chopped chives or green onions. The soup freezes really well for a future meal as well!

Sloppy Joes

Okay, I promise this is the last recipe with sweet potatoes. But it's so good! Who doesn't love sloppy joes? And I have made it better by eliminating that bad-for-you bun or bread underneath it all.

1 large sweet potato
1 tablespoon olive oil
1 tablespoon melted butter, allowed to cool slightly
½ teaspoon coarse salt
1 teaspoon freshly ground black pepper
1 lb. ground beef
1 small onion, diced
1 bell pepper (any colour), diced
2 cloves garlic, pressed or minced
1 can (150 ml) tomato paste
½ teaspoon salt
3 tablespoons honey
1 teaspoon chilli powder
2 tablespoons apple cider vinegar
1 cup water
Freshly ground black pepper to taste

Preheat oven to 375 degrees, adjusting oven rack to middle or slightly closer to bottom. Wash the sweet potatoes and cut crosswise into slices that are about ½ inch thick – you are trying to loosely resemble slices of bread, so keep that in mind at the market when picking out your vegetable! You can discard or eat raw the little ends that are too small.

Spread your cut potatoes out on a baking sheet or large baking dish. Drizzle the olive oil and butter over the sweet potatoes and then sprinkle on the salt and pepper. Flip them over a few times to get them nicely coated on both sides. Bake for 40 minutes without turning or peeking.

Now that your 'bread' is in the oven, you can concentrate on the sloppy part. Brown the ground beef in a skillet. Add the onion and peppers and sauté for a few minutes until soft. Add the garlic for the last 30 seconds.

Mix all the remaining ingredients together and add to the skillet. Let this simmer until slightly thickened but still sloppy. When your potatoes are ready, put a couple of slices on each plate and top with the meat and vegetable mixture.

33
The Grass Is Always Greener

Haven't we been told to eat our greens for decades? I certainly remember my parents force-feeding us green things like broccoli and it never really goes well with most children. It's actually a bit comforting to know this advice has remained constant for such a long time. It's just good for your body and mind!

If we step back to our earlier hunter-gatherer conversation, nature has always provided all the correct components for our human bodies in green vegetables. They help alkalize your body, just like breathing.

You can make it a bit easier on yourself if you adopt a few tricks with this. Look at your plate and try to make it colourful, and not just green, but a lot of bright colours. Les and I always know we have failed miserably at this if our plates are all brown – meat and potatoes. So remember it is just like your patch of grass; green is better and reminds us of summer and brown is bad like your grass in winter!

It's easy to add a green component to almost every meal. When you have to choose, pick the green one, with some steamed greens or a salad as a side dish and some herbs on your eggs in the morning. Perhaps Kermit, the Frog, was wrong when he sang, 'It's not easy being green'.

34
Get Cultured

I hope you are seeing a bit of a theme here with all this food talk. A lot of the recommendations I am sharing are about adding things to our diets to make our bodies and minds healthier. I have heard this referred to as, "If you add, you'll crowd."

Most of the crazy fad diets out there tend to focus on eliminating things and this can be very restrictive from a psychological state. Think about the last time you took a toy away from a child and how it suddenly became their favourite!

One of the food groups you can add to your repertoire is cultured foods. Cultured foods are preserved using a process of fermentation. My granny used to spend many days every autumn 'putting down', as she called it, vegetables from her garden and apples from her trees. Canning at home is a bit of a lost art, but you can still find lots of fermented foods at your local store and especially at farmer's markets.

Pickles, sauerkraut, yoghurt and even beer and wine are cultured foods. I absolutely love pickled carrots, hot peppers and other veggies. Kefir is a delicious fermented milk product that sort of resembles drinkable yoghurt and is wonderful with a bit of fresh fruit. And who doesn't love a cold beer on a warm day?

Fermentation improves the nutrient content of these foods. The action of the bacteria makes the minerals in cultured foods more readily available to the body. The bacteria also produce vitamins and enzymes that are beneficial for digestion.

And don't get freaked out by all this talk about bacteria! Our bodies are covered with healthy bacteria inside and out, and these foods help support it. Another saying we hear often these days is, "Healthy gut, healthy body." This is also why all those anti-bacterial soaps and wipes have fallen out of favour in the last few years – they are killing the good guys.

35
Healthy Fat?

'Fat' is not a very popular word in the English vocabulary, whether it applies to our bodies or the food we put in it. And the term healthy fat seems like the biggest oxymoron of the century!

Unfortunately, the 1980s ruined it for us and our relationship with fat. Someone decided the 'fat' in food made our bodies fat and food manufacturers hopped on the bandwagon, so to speak. Butter, one of my favourite things on earth, fell out of favour and was replaced by margarine which, as we know, more closely resembles the bottom of your shoe than a food product. And in order to make the 'low fat' food taste better, everyone added more of the one ingredient guaranteed to make you fat – sugar! What a disaster!

Thank goodness butter is back in style these days, as well as coconut oil as perfectly acceptable fats. Your body, and especially your brain, actually craves fat to keep it healthy. If you took your brain out and sat in on a table – which I don't recommend, by the way – you would see a lot of fat and water, which explains why it needs a lot of both.

Have you ever looked at a fish and thought about fat? I am guessing not, since most fish look pretty thin and fit to me! But there are lots of studies that show DHA and EPA – the two omega-3 fatty acids in fish – are more effective for humans than psychotherapy and antidepressants in treating depression. Some research has even found the fats in fish can improve symptoms of Attention Deficit Hyperactivity Disorder (ADHD) in children.

The best fish to eat are the small ones. Wild salmon and smaller fish, such as mackerel, anchovies, sardines and herring are all brimming with omega-3. You can even use the acronym SMASH to remember the names of these fish. The smaller the fish, the lower on the food chain it is and the less that it has eaten, so the amount of mercury and other toxins is minimized.

Growing up on the Canadian prairies as I did with no water in sight, we did not eat a lot of fish. Even when my father returned from a fishing trip with a prize catch, we seldom ate it because my mom refused to deal with the slimy thing. Frozen battered fish sticks were about as close as we got to eating fish, so it was many years into my adulthood until I even developed a taste for it. Fortunately though, I can get some of my omega-3 fats from supplements and that is exactly what I do.

Nuts and seeds also fall into the category of healthy fats. I keep a jar of almonds – the unsalted, unprocessed, un-sugar-coated kind – in my desk drawer for a quick snack that quickly satisfies a hungry pang. We put a few pumpkin seeds on our salad at dinner. And chia seeds are one of the best!

But I need to tell you a story about me and chia seeds. They first entered our house several years ago when my daughter Emily decided to start eating a more healthy diet. I thought they looked disgusting, like tiny black bugs. And they spilled everywhere like sand if you weren't careful. How am I doing at convincing you to try them?

Chia seeds are now my friends, since Les and I discovered a wonderful healthy dessert we have a couple of times a week – chia pudding. It's super healthy, gets some chia seeds into our bodies and, most importantly, eliminates the desire and craving to have ice-cream or cake for dessert!

Chia Pudding Parfaits

This recipe makes two large parfaits and takes only five minutes to prepare, but plan ahead as you need to let it set in the refrigerator for at least three hours before final assembly.

1 cup almond milk
1 can (400 ml) full-fat coconut milk
1 teaspoon vanilla extract
2 tablespoons honey
½ chia seeds
1 cup fresh or frozen blueberries, raspberries or strawberries (or a mixture!)
¼ cup roughly chopped raw walnuts, cashews or pecans (optional)

Put the milks, vanilla and honey and chia in dish or large measuring cup and mix together. Cover with a lid or plastic wrap and refrigerate for at least 3 hours or overnight. Once the chia seeds have developed a pudding-like texture, layer the mixture in a tall glass or bowl with your fruit, trying to get 3-4 layers of each. Top with chopped nuts, if desired.

36
Be Free

I think I will remember forever when Les and I 'hit the wall' on gluten insensitivity a few years ago. We were in the swimming pool on a hot summer day in Arizona and we were not at all enjoying the cold beers we had brought out at poolside. In fact, we ended up pouring them down the drain. A true and sad story!

For several months prior to that, Les had been getting sores in his mouth and the dentists and doctors were all baffled. I had been struggling with extreme bloating and cramps after most meals, to the point that I often looked nine-months pregnant, not a good look for an over-fifty gentleman! When we arrived home and visited our naturopathic doctor, she suggested we try a paleo diet for a few weeks and monitor the results. It worked.

A paleo diet basically eliminates a few major things from one's diet, with sugar and gluten being at the top of the list. Gluten is a protein found in grains and is what binds together bread, pasta and most baked goods. In the 'old days', we only heard about problems with gluten from people with celiac disease – an autoimmune condition where the body attacks itself when gluten is ingested. These days, at least in North America, gluten insensitivity has become almost an epidemic to the point that most packaged products and restaurant menus identify what is gluten-free.

I know how you love when I talk about our ancestors, so here I go again. The gluten in our food today is completely different from what our great grandparents would have experienced. Grains are now modified through GMOs (genetically modified organisms) and pesticides to the extent that I recently read an article that claimed mice and rats won't even go near grain that is stored after processing. Smart rodents!

Our bodies are becoming intolerant of all this stuff and we often get – wait for it – bloating, cramping, headaches and skin and mouth irritations. Some of the other symptoms include irritability, brain fog and extreme fatigue. Hmm. Do those sound a bit like the symptoms of anxiety and depression? The link between what we put in our mouths and what goes on in our brains cannot be overstated.

Some experts are now saying that nobody should be eating the gluten now present in our food, at least in North America. When Les and I travel to Europe, however, we seem to be able to enjoy the bread and pasta there, with no challenges. The processing is very different there. So if you do choose to eat grains, look for ones from trusted GMO-free sources.

37
Sugar Scares

If it's confession time, then I will be the first to admit I have a sweet tooth. Heck, I have a whole sweet body! I love a sugary snack better than anyone and came by it quite naturally from a young age.

My mom almost always made dessert for our evening meal. And if she didn't specifically make something, there was always ice-cream treats at the ready in the freezer. We also had a bucket of chocolate bars in our hallway linen closet too. And before you judge the location, remember we lived in a very small house and things got stored wherever there was room. Oddly enough, everyone in the family showed amazing self-control and did not eat all the treats in one sitting.

I also remember from a very young age and with my first small allowance, heading almost daily to the corner grocery store to buy 'penny candy' – and in those days, you could walk away with a nice little paper bag of yumminess for a very low investment. I loved cola too, and would sneak a sip from my father's half-used bottle in the fridge. Cola, and soft drinks in general, became quite a habit for me and my daughters still joke about how I would ask them to bring me a few cans when I was busy with a household project or cutting the grass. I drank *many* cans each day.

So now that we have established my love of sugar, you can imagine how hard it is for me to eliminate it from my diet. When our naturopathic doctor first suggested, as I mentioned earlier, that Les and I adopt the paleo diet, we had no idea what we were getting ourselves into on the sugar front. It's in everything!

It was a miracle an innocent stranger was not harmed in our first grocery shopping trip, as we walked aisle to aisle reading food labels and panicking that we would never eat again if we had to avoid sugar. Thank goodness I had already kicked the soft drink habit prior to this or you might have read about me in the newspaper.

Since you already know how I like to talk about our hunter-gatherer ancestors, let's go there for a minute. They ate the equivalent of about 80 grams (less than 1/6 pound) of sugar in a whole year, usually when they came across some fruit or berries. Sweet things from the land were safe for them to eat and are a quick source of energy that helps us store fat for times of scarcity – a concern all our brains have shared down through the ages.

The average North American today, however, consumes about 68 kilograms (150 pounds) in a year. Yikes! It's such a part of our food world that it's almost impossible to avoid unless you are a trained sleuth. And our brains haven't figured out that we don't quite need *that* much stored for a future famine.

One of the biggest challenges with *finding* all the sugar in your food is the complicated way it is identified on food labels. And this was part of our challenge at the grocery store for those first few visits. Glucose, fructose, dextrose, maltodextrin, corn syrup, fruit juice, cane sugar and agave nectar. They are all sugar.

But let's get back to why all this sugar is bad for us. Besides giving our bodies the signal to store fat for the future, it causes inflammation. And there are all kinds of studies now about how inflammation is the root cause of major illnesses from heart disease to diabetes and cancer, as well as depression and anxiety.

As we have already established, I am no saint when it comes to sugar and my journey is still in its infancy. I prefer to get a bit of a sugar from a special treat like a bowl of fruit and yoghurt or a big-old chocolate bar rather than all throughout my day in everything else I eat. It seems pretty logical to stop putting too much of something in my mouth that is going to make me fat, sad and sick.

38
Visualize

Do you ever wonder why your parents and teachers got upset with you for using profanity or bad language? It relates to that whole idea of garbage in equalling garbage out.

Each one of us has about sixty thousand thoughts a day. We are constantly receiving messages from the environment around us and processing those messages either consciously or subconsciously. So if we are bombarded by bad stuff we hear or see, even it is coming out of our own mouths, it should be no surprise when bad stuff results for us.

Every thought either moves you toward your goal of being a better, healthier person or moves you away from it. So it benefits us greatly if we can try to control at least *some* of those thousands of thoughts. Our bodies can even heal themselves, physically and emotionally, with the right building blocks of thought. A bit of a mind shift has to happen first.

Since Les and I travel quite often, we also often find ourselves stressing out about delayed flights and missed connections to other flights. If we can stop ourselves and focus our energy on imagining reaching our destination successfully, everything changes for the better. I often get myself worked up about upcoming meetings or presentations, but if I can visualize it going very well, it usually does just that.

If thinking and imagining the best in your mind is the way to go, then it makes sense that putting positive images in front of your eyes will also help. We have a vision board in our house, right above where our computer sits actually, so we see it many times a day. On it are magazine clippings and photographs of the things we want to achieve and the places we want to visit.

Having a vision board doesn't need to be complicated or fancy. It could be a few photos or clippings pinned to the side of your bathroom mirror where you brush your teeth or style your hair. Or it could be the most common and age-old bulletin board in most homes – the front of the refrigerator.

I challenge you to give it a try. Put up a photo of the car you want to drive, the house you want to live in or the beach you want to sit upon and see if your thoughts help you move toward those things. What not to post on your board? This month's electricity bill or your child's less-than-perfect report card.

39
Be Still, Be Quiet

I have written before about the old adage that our Creator gave us two eyes, two ears and one mouth for a good reason – we are meant to spend a lot more time watching and listening than we do speaking. I will admit I am on the far side of this equation and prefer to look and listen rather than speak.

I read recently that women speak an average of seven thousand words per day while men come in at about two thousand words. I offer no gender-based judgement on this statistic except to say that I have witnessed it as absolutely accurate in my thirty-plus years of office employment where women made up the majority of the workforce. And a family dinner with my daughters is exactly the same!

So, since I can only offer an opinion from my own experience and gender, I place a great deal of importance on quiet, peaceful thought and the use of very few words to get my point across, except when it comes to writing and this book apparently!

In terms of anxiety, I find it a lot less stressful to quietly contemplate things and use a few words than to feel I have to prepare a lengthy epistle or diatribe.

40
Run for Your Life

Have you ever watched kids run? We all have for sure, but it's interesting to step back and think about that action a bit. Children run without giving it a second thought. It's just a faster way to get somewhere or to something than by walking. They don't worry about falling, breaking a hip or scratching their knees or noses.

I used to hate it when my little daughters ran. I was the one afraid they would fall and scratch a knee or nose or, worse yet, break a bone. As adults, some of us have learned to be anxious and afraid of a lot of normal things that children do quite naturally.

Young children laugh when they are happy and cry when they are sad. And they scream when they are angry! When they are frightened, they come to their mom or dad or grandparent for help and may want to just be held tightly until they feel safe again. They might even curl up in a ball.

After children feel comforted and have expressed their feelings – which usually doesn't take very long – they are over it. They then run happily back to their play and are happy again.

We all can't pretend we're children again, but there are definitely some lessons here we can apply. Run more – or at least get out and take a walk. Laugh when you're happy and cry when you're sad. Even if you have to go outside, scream when you're angry! Talk to someone you love when you're scared. And remember, most of all, we all get scared.

41
Grandma Knows Best

For the first nine years of my life, my maternal grandmother – Granny, we called her – lived just two houses down from us on the same street. It was the perfect situation for my parents having an almost built-in babysitter and an equally perfect situation for my sisters and me as we got to spend a lot of time at her house.

Granny taught me so many things in the short time we had together on this earth and I was devastated when she passed away with cancer. In hindsight, much of what she taught me was the good old basics on reducing anxiety and worry in my life.

Since she worked fulltime at a job, Saturday was Granny's shopping day and she almost always took me along. Our little secret was I could put almost anything I wanted in the shopping cart and she would keep it at her house for when I came over. In doing that, she created an atmosphere of comfort at her home and I learned by default not to overindulge on candy and treats because there was never any shortage.

Granny also got us started on drinking tea at very young ages. We would drink it from fancy teacups with milk and sugar added. And since it was very hot, we took lots of time letting it cool and enjoying it slowly. I still enjoy a cup of tea many times a day and it almost always slows me down and helps me think. I'm drinking a cup as I write this.

Something else Granny taught me was to have no judgment on other people, although I'm not sure I understood the lesson until much later in my life. She had a small suite in her basement that she rented out and every one of her tenants became like family, even though the colour of their skin or their backgrounds were not always the same as ours. She even travelled to Spain and Japan with one of the ladies, something that was not that common in the 1960s, and I received a very early introduction to a love of travel.

And on the subject of not judging, my sisters and I would spend hours playing in her bedroom and dressing up in beautiful dresses and piling on the costume jewellery. No comments please! I did not develop a penchant for wearing women's clothes, but what I did learn was to have some good fun with my imagination.

42
Read

I have heard it said that a requirement of putting words out is to first bring them in. JK Rowling, famous for her *Harry Potter* book series, said it succinctly, "The most important thing is to read as much as you can, like I did. It will give you an understanding of what makes good writing and it will enlarge your vocabulary." Ernest Hemmingway said it even better when he wrote, "There is no friend as loyal as a book."

I usually have at least two books on the go at all times – one having something to do with business or learning a new skill and the other for pure enjoyment. On a recent family trip to Italy over Christmas, my daughters and son-in-law brought many volumes with them to pass the time in the car, at train stations and in front of the fire in the evenings. It made me quite proud!

Books allow you to escape into another place without the need for artificial stimulation from the many electronic devices available to us today. It's a wonderful way to reduce stress, be still and eliminate anxiety. And if you have even a small library near you, you can enjoy as many books as you like for no cost. What's more perfect than that?

Reading books allows you to check the facts, so to speak, and compare multiple viewpoints. As I have said before, I am not an expert on anything I have written in this book. But I watch many documentaries, numerous webcasts and read a lot of books. If I have said something here, it is because I have heard it or read it multiple times. But do your own research. Make your own decisions.

43
Ground Is Good

One of the great things about writing this book is the many things I learned along the way. It never ceases to amaze me how we can live decades in this world and have not even heard about the hundreds of ways our body can heal itself.

The ancient wisdom of grounding falls into this category for me. Grounding is also known as earthing and you might hate me for going there again, but it takes us back to our hunter-gatherer ancestors and their lack of fashionable footwear.

Most of us, at least where I come from where it is cold and snowy for more than half of the year, wear shoes or boots for a very high percentage of our day. I'm not sure I have a choice! And that footwear has rubber or plastic soles which are insulating us from mother earth.

The earth is actually like a six trillion-ton metric battery. Who knew? This battery is constantly being replenished by lightning and solar radiation. And since all of our body's energy, movements, emotions and behaviours come from electrical energy, we get 'grounded' when our bare feet connect with the earth and its magnetic field. Like charging the battery in your phone or any of your other cordless appliances, it occurs from our feet up, feeding the trillions of cells in our body.

All of this magnetic field stuff is well-recognized by the scientific and medical profession. When I had chronic back and sciatic pain a few years ago, my naturopathic doctor suggested I buy magnetic insoles for my shoes. At first, I thought I might stick to metal objects as I walked by, but they are not that strong! They obviously have just enough magnetic energy to 'recharge' my nerves and muscles, and the pain disappeared.

At my daughter's outdoor wedding two summers ago, she and all of her female wedding party wore beautiful lace wraps on their feet, but they were basically barefoot in the grass for the ceremony, photos and reception. The day turned out to be highly dramatic with lots of family turmoil occurring, but they all remained perfectly calm and collected. Coincidence?

Although I have not camped outdoors in a tent for many years, I remember always having the best night's sleep despite lying without much between me and the hard ground. Earthing at its best.

New parents often tell stories of their babies and episodes of colic, but evidence shows that holding a baby outside with your bare feet on the ground can calm a child better than anything else. Likely not during a Canadian winter, but I digress!

Experts in the field recommend at least twenty minutes a day outside with your shoes off. This can be a great time for a little breath work, meditation and some gratitude review too. Heck, if you really want to return to your ancestral roots, pick some berries while you are out there! The immediate result is improved blood flow and ultimately an end to aches, pains and overall improved health.

44
Forest Freshness

Since we're talking about the earth and how connecting to it benefits our mind and body, it's worth a quick segue into the topic of forest bathing. I have to thank my friend Karen for this one as, even though I had done it for years as a child, I did not know there was a term for it!

When I was growing up, our family was lucky enough to have a cabin in the mountains about one hour west of our home. My grandfather and father built it from a kit around the time I was born and it was pretty rustic and tucked away in the woods. Although we always had electricity, we didn't have running water until many years later when we drilled a water well and put in a septic system. It's been completely modernized now and is still my father's home.

In the early days, my sisters and I would play in the woods for hours. There was a narrow, well-worn path through the trees leading to a back corner of the property and there, we had made log furniture and used some of my mom's old pots for a pretend kitchen. When my sisters grew up and stopped coming to the cabin, I claimed the space and even made a wood sign proclaiming it 'Ken's Korner'.

So as you can probably tell, the concept of forest bathing has nothing to do with water. It is all about soaking in the healing properties of trees and plants. Most people don't have their own corner of the woods in which to play pretend chef and make endless mud pies as I did all those years ago. But a slow, deliberate, meditative walk in the woods can offer many mental, emotional and physical benefits.

It's based on the Japanese practice of shinrin-yoku, which translates to 'taking in the forest atmosphere'. It goes without saying – I hope – that no cellphones, devices or music-making equipment are allowed on this journey. And if you recall my explanation of 'no-equipment required' workouts, this is one of the reasons I love the whole idea of forest bathing.

All you have to do – once you have found a patch of forest, that is – is to take your time and notice the sights, sounds and smells around you. If you are sharing this with another person, commit to each other that you will not speak for this part of your adventure so you can both enjoy it in your own way. As you relax, you will almost instantly feel your worries slip away.

Along with your disappearing worries, it's likely you will also experience reduced blood pressure, an increased energy level, an overall sense of happiness and will arrive home that evening to much-improved sleep. You can even combine this therapy with some grounding if there is a place along the way to slip off your shoes and connect with the forest floor.

45
Comfort Cures

Although I recommend a 'clean' diet to keep our bodies and our minds healthy, I also believe certain times call for special food. And please do not call it cheating, because that just adds more anxiety and guilt that none of us need. I also really dislike the term, 'eating our emotions'.

Many foods are referred to as 'comfort foods' for the basic reason that they bring you comfort! A big bowl of popcorn shared in front of the fire or a movie, a hot cup of freshly-brewed coffee or hot chocolate consumed with a friend or loved one and a favourite recipe that reminds you of something your mother made many years ago. These are things that bring us joy and should definitely be part of our lives when needed.

Holidays are a very good example of a time when tradition and comfort trumps healthy and lean. And why not? These times are usually to celebrate something traditional and to bring family and friends together. In most cultures, this involves food in a major way.

In general, Les and I eat a gluten-free diet with a high percentage of vegetables at our house, but that doesn't mean I don't put together a fantastic bread stuffing at Christmas time. Les is not a fan of turkey, but we still put a giant bird in the oven as the centerpiece of a big family dinner because it brings comfort and tradition to the family table. And he loves to bake dozens of fancy cookies at the holidays to share and some of them do find their way to our own tummies.

Over time, we have learned to make our favourite comfort foods just a little healthier while maintaining the great taste.

But I also believe that everything in moderation is the way to go. If you're feeling sad – or happy for that matter – and need a piece of chocolate, you should go for it.

We try to pair a green salad with dinner almost every night, but love a salad dressing with a little more 'oomph' or comfort-level than vinaigrette. Here's Les' now-famous healthy Thousand Island dressing recipe.

Thousand Island Salad Dressing/Dip

The homemade mayo can be used for other recipes too!

4 egg yolks
4 teaspoons lemon juice
4 teaspoons hot mustard
1 cup avocado oil

Put in a tall container with oil on top. Use a hand blender and process until creamy!

To make the Thousand Island dressing, add the full mayo recipe to:

4 tablespoons sugar-free ketchup
2 tablespoons white vinegar
8-10 chopped dill pickles (sugar-free)

Mix and refrigerate. Yum! If you have trouble finding sugar-free ketchup for this recipe (that high-fructose corn syrup is awfully bad for you!), here's an easy way to make your own.

Simple Ketchup

1 can (150 ml) tomato paste
2 tablespoons white vinegar
1/3 cup water
¼ teaspoon dry mustard
¼ teaspoon cinnamon
¼ teaspoon salt
1 pinch of ground cloves
1 pinch of ground allspice

Whisk all the ingredients together in a bowl or measuring cup and refrigerate.

Guacamole

Take two avocados, cut in half lengthwise, with pits and skin removed.
1 small white, yellow or red onion, diced
1 jalapeno pepper, stem removed and diced (leave seeds in if you like it hot)
1 tomato, diced
½ fresh lime, squeezed (or 1 tablespoon lime juice)
½ teaspoon sea salt

Combine all the ingredients in a molcajete or bowl, mashing and mixing them together. It's best to leave a few lumps in the avocado if you can. Some people add some freshly chopped cilantro at the end but, once again, we are not fans of cilantro, so skip this step.

You can refrigerate the guacamole for a few hours before serving, but it's best to use it up as quickly as possible. Put one or both of the avocado pits back onto the top of your bowl to keep it from turning brown before you enjoy it.

I'm sorry, but I could not walk away from a chapter on comfort food without talking about pizza. And since it's the ultimate comfort food only when it comes from a pizzeria to your door with almost no effort on your part, that's where I am focusing.

Les happens to love cold leftover pizza the next day, but I have never been a fan. Reheating it always paled in comparison to the fresh product, however, until I found the great trick I am about to share. The microwave makes it soggy and a hot oven dries it out, so what is one to do?

Re-heating Leftover Pizza

Place as many of your cold slices as you want on a baking sheet and cover the sheet tightly with aluminum foil. Put the sheet on the lowest possible rack of a cold oven. Now set the oven temperature to 275 degrees and let the pizza warm for 25-30 minutes.

This amazing little trick works because it reverses the crystallization of the starch in the crust that happened overnight in the refrigerator. As the pizza warms up, the crystals release the trapped moisture again and soften the crust. The sealed sheet keeps the slices from drying out and putting it low in the oven means the crust crisps up before the toppings start to shrivel.

The only thing you have to remember to do now is to order enough pizza so you have some leftovers for the next day!

46
Just Go Play

My mom was famous for telling us to "Just go play," when she wanted us out from under foot or to stop fighting with each other over some insignificant thing. It turns out it was great advice. But for some reason, we stop playing when we grow up – at least play for play's sake.

As adults, we somehow transition into a world where we are not supposed to play but instead, we spend our time worrying and stressing out about everyday problems. Every activity has to have an end result – we go to our jobs to earn money. We exercise to lose weight and we 'network' with other people to move our careers ahead instead of just spending some fun time with them.

My partner, Les, loves to bake and is really good at doing this just because he likes it. We try to eat a paleo diet and baking is not terribly exciting without the usual flour and sugar ingredients. But that doesn't stop him from baking up delicious treats – for the fun of it – which we then take to our respective offices for others to enjoy.

The trick is making sure we make time in our days for some play before there is no time left. Many of us have seen the demonstration where the professor fills the jar with large rocks, pebbles and sand to show this concept. If you haven't ever seen it, let me try to explain it in words.

If the things that are most important to you like your family, your health and your passions are the big rocks, you can put those easily in the jar and it looks full. You can then add some pebbles to represent some of the other 'stuff' like work and school so that it fills in all the spaces. Finally, although the jar appears quite full already, you can pour in some sand that will completely fill in the gaps – things like cleaning the house, paying bills and expanding your shoe collection.

But if you 'fill your jar' (or your days) with the pebbles and sand, there will not be enough room for the big rocks. Your family, health and play will suffer and not 'fit' into your life. What a great lesson!

So go for that long walk, bake that cake and write that letter to your grandmother before you work late one more night and post your hundredth shoe photo on Instagram.

47
There's Only One You

If you work at a regular job like I do, there is usually an annual torture mechanism in place referred to as a performance review. This is the day each year where your supervisor or boss gets to tell you, from their point of view, how wonderful or horrible you are at your job. And there's usually some paperwork involved so it can be captured for all eternity.

Now most proponents of this process will tell you that you should never wait until review time to discuss the really good or bad stuff, as that should be handled all through the year as it occurs. The problem is human nature causes that to rarely happen.

As an anxious person, I do not usually relish review time and don't really know that many people that do enjoy it. I can recall vividly some of my more memorable ones over the years.

In one of my first roles in the public relations area of a large oil and gas company, I had the pleasure of working for a woman who was rather particular about the ways things were done, shall we say. I will always remember – which in itself is a bit disturbing – how she would handwrite a note to the secretary (yes, they were called that) to instruct her to staple or three-hole punch the piece of paper to which the note was attached.

In one of my first performance reviews with this individual, she noted I was far too self-effacing and should go about improving this. I had absolutely no idea what this meant and, since there was no *Google* back then, I had to turn to a large dictionary in the office to find the meaning. I learned it meant I was reserved, shy, timid or modest. This did not come as a shock to me!

What was disturbing, however, was that in bringing this to my attention, she actually thought it could change my personality. So I worried and fretted about this for most of my career there, taking courses and reading books on how to be *less* self-effacing. Guess what? It didn't work.

Certainly, I have improved my skills in many areas and even learned to quite enjoy speaking in front of a group of people. But I also learned my personality is what makes me unique and, well, me!

In re-reading the definition of self-effacing now, I am reminded it also means 'tending to make oneself or one's actions inconspicuous, especially because of humility and typically giving credit to the other players'. Hmm. Yes, that's me. And I'm quite proud of it.

In my current office, I am fortunate to work with a wide variety of people of different ages and from different backgrounds. It's actually one of the things for which I am truly grateful when I take the time to count my blessings. But I was disturbed recently when a couple of the ladies were called out about some personal habits.

One has a loud and infectious laugh that can be heard throughout the office and is constantly reminded how distracting this is. The other individual types very loudly on her computer keyboard as she produces a great deal of output – to the point that her workspace partner actually bought her a rubber keyboard.

How sad it is to me that these two productive and pleasant people cannot go about their business *and* exhibit some quirky traits. These pieces of their personality make them exactly who they are and should not be identified as faults.

We have all heard the medical statistics of how completely unique each one of us is, since millions of sperm have to compete to fertilize the egg that begins our lives. So why do we spend so much of our lives trying to be someone we are not? We try to look like the person in the magazine, act like the person on television or write like the famous author – believe me when I say I have tried the latter and it does not work.

When I was a teenager, one of the songs I loved most from the *Bee Gees* was called 'Be Who You Are', and the lyrics are as relevant to me today as they were all those years ago. The first stanza says:

Be who you are,
Don't ever change,
The world was made to measure for your smile,
So smile.

48
Don't Fail to Share

The world is full of catchy sayings like "Nobody's perfect" and "We learn from our mistakes", but we all know that success is the ultimate goal and failure can be downright embarrassing and anxiety-causing. We think that being strong and pretending like everything is perfect is the way to go.

But have you ever noticed how, even though our failures can be devastating to us, they become far less important as soon as you share it with someone else? Keeping a mistake a secret and hoping no one else will notice just makes it worse and continues to make it bigger than reality in your mind.

The other great thing about sharing a failure with someone else is the almost instant bond you create with that person. They see you as a real person and may even share a similar failure with you – or better yet, a solution they found that worked for them.

49
Boredom is Bad

Do kids still utter that annoying phrase, "I'm bored," expecting an adult to miraculously find an engaging activity for them? I know I said this plenty of times as a little kid and was usually told to go play outside or something equally cliché. We didn't have a dozen electronic gadgets to occupy our time and that was probably a good thing. Sometimes it was hard work to find something to do with ourselves, especially if no friends or other family was available.

Many years ago when my partner, Les, was employed in the investment area of a large bank, he barely had enough work to keep him occupied beyond the first hour of the day. He spent the rest of the day surfing the internet and being nearly bored out of his mind. Not surprisingly, his employment there did not last beyond a few months before he had to move on.

We human beings need to be busy in order to be happy. We already know that our body will age faster and get more aches and pains when we don't get it moving regularly with exercise and activities. The same can be said for our brain – it needs to be stimulated.

Have you ever noticed how tired you feel coming home from a boring day at your job, or one where you did not accomplish anything, versus one where you did forty-six things? Although none of us likes to be overwhelmed by too much work, we seem to thrive on being active and busy.

The best days on a weekend for me are when I suddenly notice that the clock says 4:00 p.m. and I have not yet showered or combed my hair! It feels so good to be busy, even if it is just a few household chores.

I like to go to bed quite early, get 8-9 hours of sleep and rise early – and I get a bit out-of-sorts when this schedule is disrupted. But it always amazes me how I can stay up late and get much less sleep in my peak season at work each summer when I am required to be onsite for eighteen hours a day or more. I have an abundance of energy because I am excited and have worked toward the event all year long.

This story played out for Les and me a few years ago when we visited Italy as part of a Mediterranean cruise. After enjoying nearly unlimited fine and rich food on the ship, we suddenly and rather unexpectedly found ourselves hiking the famous trail at Cinque Terre. We are not regular hikers and did not train for such an activity, but nevertheless were high above the sea teetering up and down rocky slopes and right through the middle of wet and slippery olive groves and vineyards. The scenery was breathtaking and our bodies rose to the occasion!

We can't always travel to exotic destinations to get our minds and bodies engaged, but there is another trick that works amazingly well when we are stuck in a less-than-perfect situation. Act like you are enjoying it, even if you're not.

If you go to a movie where you dislike the lead actor, you will not like the movie no matter how wonderful it might be. If you go to a bad movie where you like the actor, chances are that you will still enjoy it. Are you following me? Obviously we should all strive to find a life that provides us with enough interesting things to keep us getting out of bed in the morning. But when boring things happen, we can make the best of them by 'changing our minds', so to speak.

The Philosopher and Roman Emperor Marcus Aurelius may have explained it best when he said, "Our life is what our thoughts make it."

50
Sleep It Off

I have written before about my mom and how she was able to function on very little sleep. At least it seemed that way to me. She would sit up late at night balancing the family budget, reading novels and watching crime shows on television – and almost always with a cigarette in her hand and a cup of coffee nearby. Then she would be up again long before the rest of us, preparing a hot breakfast and getting bagged lunches ready. Not exactly a recipe for healthy living!

I do know that she was a napper, however, so she got some much-needed rest when all of us were away at school and work. I read recently how John D. Rockefeller, one of the richest men ever, took naps after lunch and dinner. And Winston Churchill would apparently remain in bed until 11:00 a.m. doing paperwork, but dozed off when he got tired – *and* he still had an afternoon nap.

Many cultures incorporate an afternoon break, nap or siesta into their day, often even closing down businesses for a few hours to allow for this. We North Americans, however, seem to treat our busy lives and lack of sleep like badges of honour.

There is no need to take my word for the value of sleep, since most doctors and many medical journals speak of its value. And don't forget that mind-boggling statistic about how we spend one-third of our lives in bed, based on eight hours of sleep each night.

The challenge, however, is that many of us do not get enough sleep. Certainly I was guilty of this in my younger days of late-night studying, socializing and later on being up at all hours with young children. I simply can't function on less than eight hours now and make sure that my life and social plans allow for this.

Sleep rejuvenates brain cells, heals the body and reduces anxiety. Consider it your mind's digestion time. In Canada, we have a semi-annual adjustment of the clocks backwards and forwards called 'daylight savings' to allow for more light in the evenings. It's a great study on the need for sleep, since more accidents and illnesses occur in the week after we set our clocks ahead than the whole rest of the year because of the 'loss' of the hour.

You can also improve the quality and duration of your sleep by making some changes to the 'bookends' of your day and your sleeping environment. It is well documented now that our televisions and portable devices emit a blue light that messes up our ability to fall asleep, so these should be avoided right before bed. I never understood anyway how anyone would want to watch all the horrible things on the evening news right before trying to sleep! Eating or drinking within a few hours of bedtime should also be avoided so your stomach is done with all its work before you lie down.

It helps our bodies if we can get closer to the natural light and dark rhythms of the universe as well. Does that sound too abstract? The invention of artificial light may have been the single-biggest enemy of our sleep patterns, since our ancestors basically slept when it got dark and woke when it was light again. You can adjust this in your home by having various types of lighting or dimmable lighting and softening the light levels as you get closer to bedtime.

You want to make sure your bedroom is dark enough too – we used to put aluminum foil on my daughters' bedroom windows to make it totally dark, especially when bedtime was before sunset. And get the temperature right – we like it cold in the room with a big, fluffy duvet to keep us warm – but everyone has their own preferences.

51
Keep It Moving

Earlier in these pages, I told you about how I was never very good at team sports as a kid and that theme has continued well into my life as an adult. It has just never been my thing! But that doesn't mean I have ignored the importance of keeping my body moving. Nowhere is the term 'use it or lose it' more appropriate.

So with my disinterest in team sports as a given, over the years I have tried having a gym membership and my own fitness equipment at home in order to stay in shape. I would be embarrassed to calculate the amount of money wasted on both. The only bright sides were some fortunate gym owners who never saw my face and still collected my money and a few other lucky people who walked away with pristine unused equipment when I finally gave in and sold it.

For me, a short daily stretching and exercise routine first thing in the morning and a decent amount of walking throughout the remainder of the day is perfect. Everyone is different. The goal for which you should strive is to create a customized plan for movement that works for *you*. Maybe it's dancing, yoga, soccer, hiking, biking or playing street hockey with the kids after dinner. Even cleaning your house counts!

I was in the best condition of my life as a teenager with a part-time job, carrying out groceries to people's cars. I walked for a living. I walked to work, walked in and out of the store all day long and then walked home. These days, there are thousands of books, websites and doctor shows talking about the benefits of walking. Human beings have been doing it since time began and it doesn't require any equipment or training!

My short stretching and exercise routine each morning is the same – no equipment required. I do some basic stretches while I am still in the shower. It's safer to stretch muscles when they are a bit warm already. Then after my shower, I do some push-ups, triceps dips and deep knee squats – the latter because I read an article about how the single-biggest reason elderly people end up needing to move to care facilities is because they cannot get themselves down and up off the toilet!

The walking part of my day is also perfect for me because I find it to be something I can do exactly at my own pace, choosing my own route and even the desired amount of time. I get really sad when I cannot get my walk into my day, mostly because of our Canadian weather. So I try to be creative and walk inside where I work or up and down the stairs at home.

You don't need to run marathons. A walk around the block after dinner or a lunchtime stroll will do the trick. Most 'experts' say thirty minutes each day is enough and it can even be broken into three walks for ten minutes. Take the stairs, park far away from where you are going and just go for a walk!

It is also very gratifying to use technology to track your steps, since almost every smartphone has a step-counter on it now or you can get those fancy wrist computers to do it. Challenge yourself to beat your daily average or all-time record. Doing ten thousand steps per day seems to be the new norm.

The most important thing is that you move more in order to help your body oxygenate and promote cellular health. Movement does more than just help heal your body. It also boosts your hope and joy for life and combats anxiety and depression. One thing is for sure – a sedentary life is as deadly as smoking, chronic stress and a fast-food diet.

52
First Place

Prior to a recent trip to Italy, Les and I decided to take an evening class to learn how to speak Italian. It ended up being pretty intense, since neither of us had any background in the language and the teacher took it pretty seriously. Some weeks, it would cross my mind that it would be easier to just skip the class and avoid the stress of it all! We're adults after all. There were no grades involved, and so who would care? But is avoidance really the way to beat anxiety?

I went to every class faithfully and, by the end of the course, there were only four of us left. I was so glad I hung in there and have tried to keep up with my studies in Italian every day since. It's easy to be tempted to use terms like teacher's pet or brown-noser in classroom situations like this, but I might remind you these are the negative views of taking responsibility.

Being chronically late, either with your physical presence or with your work and responsibilities, can create anxiety that is just not necessary. I am almost always one of the first people in the office in the morning and find it incredibly liberating to be able to get a head start on my day with no interruptions, except for the string of texts and emails from other people saying they are running late, that is. That's too much stress for me!

When something is due to your teacher, professor or boss, I recommend you be the first one to hand it in. This is one area where it pays to win the race. Do it often and you will be remembered for being the first, even if your submission is not perfect.

In my experience as both a boss and a subordinate, no one wants to spend time reminding people over and over to show up on time for work or meetings, or to hand something in. But punctuality and a quick response is always appreciated and remembered.

In the new millennium, this goes for responding to text messages and emails also. Even if you don't have the exact or immediate answer to someone's question or enquiry, responding quickly with "I will check and get right back to you" will win you points every time.

53
The Roller Coaster

All these words I have written about identifying and reducing our anxiety and fear might lead you to believe the ideal life is one where we are floating happily from one positive experience to another as we go down the path of life. But nothing could be further from the truth.

We need the ups and downs of life. We need the good days and the not-so-good days. How else would we recognize the good parts if we didn't experience the crummy parts?

In order to enjoy that festive holiday meal laid out on a beautifully decorated table, we have to stress out a little about what to cook, the prices at the grocery store and how it is all going to fit in the oven at once. And where is everyone going to sit if Aunt Winnie shows up?

In order to see the smile on someone's face when they open a gift, you need to take the time to make it or shop for it and worry, just a little, if they will like it. The human experience is nothing if not complicated.

The trick for us all is to recognize, like a roller coaster, the downs are always going to be followed with some ups. And if we keep our bodies healthy and well-maintained, the machine will not break down on one of those lows and leave us stranded at the amusement park still buckled into our seat.

54
Love, Love, Love

Can't you just hear *The Beatles* singing those lyrics in their famous song *All You Need is Love*? And here we are at the fifty-fourth chapter of a book by a fifty-four-year-old guy – dad, son, brother, husband and friend – who just hopes the world could show more love.

It's pretty simplistic, but I really do believe the world would have a lot less fear, stress, anxiety and depression if we all chose love over hate more often and if we chose the truth over gossip, the good in others rather than the bad and adopted that good-old attitude of the glass half-full instead of half-empty.

We all smile in the same language. A smile opens doors and breaks down barriers in every corner of the world. Why not be the smiling, loving person in every room you enter? It just might help you – or someone else that needs it – make lemonade out of the lemons life sometimes give us, just like that poster on my childhood bedroom wall proclaimed all those years ago.

Conclusion

One of the visions I had for this book was to provide a really simple guide to help you come to a place where you are able to manage your well-being effectively on your own. A place where you do not need help from a doctor or therapist. A place where, when you get out of bed each morning, you want and choose to do more things that help you feel well and be happy.

I'm just one average guy who has lived through a few decades of a life laden with worry and anxiety. And make no mistake – I have had a pretty amazing life and plan to be around for at least as long all over again. But I hope that by reading some of my crazy stories, you might lessen your own worry and anxiety in ways I have tried out personally.

We all have the ability to heal ourselves. If you cut your finger, it heals. We can heal our brains too. Do you know that depression is not the cause of your sadness and despair? It's a label we have developed so it can be treated with medication called an anti-depressant. Complicated stuff, eh?

Anxiety is also not a thing. It is a symptom of stress or other things occurring in your life that pull you away from a healthy and happy existence.

If you take anything away when you put this book down, I hope it is the inclination to develop habits, habits and more habits. They now say the old rule of it taking twenty-one days to form a habit is just a myth, because it is different for everyone. But if it takes you thirty-five days, is that so awful?

Drinking water when rising, moving and exercising your body, breathing and meditation, being close to the earth and out in the sun, having good food choices and good digestion, getting enough rest. Do those all sound like hobbies you can embrace until they become such a part of your day that you hardly even notice them anymore?

Many people have asked how I ever found the time to write two books. I write at least five hundred words each day before I do anything else. It's just another habit, another hobby.

Since you have now read this book, I'm guessing you are the type of person – like me – that listens to advice, attends or watches seminars and reads a lot. I'll also hazard a guess that you don't often hear or read something that is brand-new information you have never heard before. We all *know* what we need to do to eat healthier and develop great relationships. We all *know* how to spend our money more wisely and live simpler lives.

So, all we have to do is do what we already know to do! We don't need to wait to start until we are older, taller or better-looking. Start today.

And remember to not beat yourself up when things fall off the rails, so to speak. I am the master of the system and routine and doing the same thing over and over. But one day of not writing, working out or eating perfectly will not matter. Each morning when you rise, you have a brand-new page and what you did or did not do yesterday no longer matters.

At the beginning of this journey with you, I said I wasn't an expert on any of this and I doubt you are either! But here we are at the end and hopefully we're all a little better for having thought about a few things differently.

I often find words we can all live by in poems and songs. Hedley, a western Canadian pop-rock group, says it best in this case with the lyrics from their song *Perfect*:

"I'm not perfect
But I keep trying
'Cause that's what I said I would do from the start."